Stefan Bergmann/Christian Butz

Adventure Sports

BIG FOOT

A Complete Guide

Meyer & Meyer Sport

Original title: Big foot : der neue Skispaß
© 1997 by Meyer & Meyer Verlag, Aachen/Germany
Translated by James Beachus

Die Deutsche Bibliothek - CIP-Einheitsaufnahme

Bergmann, Stefan:
Big foot : A Complete Guide / Stefan Bergmann ; Christian Butz.
[Transl.: James Beachus]. – Aachen : Meyer und Meyer, 1999
Dt. Ausg. u.d.T.: Bergmann, Stefan: Big Foot
ISBN 3-89124-497-5

All rights reserved. Except for use in a review, no part of this publication may be reproduced, stored in a retrieval system, or transmitted, in any form or by any means now known or hereafter invented without the prior written permission of the publisher. This book may not be lent, resold, hired out or otherwise disposed of by way of trade in any form, binding or cover other than that which is published, without the prior written consent of the publisher.

© 1999 by Meyer & Meyer Sport, Aachen
Olten (CH), Vienna, Oxford,
Québec, Lansing/ Michigan, Adelaide, Auckland, Johannesburg
Translation: James Beachus
Editors: John Cughlan, Dr. Irmgard Jaeger
Cover photos: Stefan Bergmann; Christian Butz, Mülheim a d. Ruhr
Figures: Michael Menzel, Neukirchen-Vluyn
Cover design: Walter J. Neumann, N&N Design-Studio, Aachen
Cover exposure: frw, Reiner Wahlen, Aachen
Printed and bound in Germany by
Druckpunkt Offset GmbH, Bergheim
e-mail: verlag@meyer-meyer-sports.com • http://www.meyer-meyer-sports.com
ISBN 3-89124-497-5

INDEX

1. **Getting Started** 9

2. **Mental Preparation** 11
   BIG FOOT: A Big Deal? – Last Chance 11

3. **Introduction to the 'Foot'** 15
   Anatomy 15
   Handling 19
   Characteristics and Types of Use 24

4. **BIG FOOT – Fun for the Children (and not only them)** 27
   Winter Sports with the Offspring:
   How Do I Turn My Children into 'Slippery Slopers'? 27

5. **In the Beginning there was the Foot –
   The Alternative Beginner's Course** 35
   A 'Recipe' for Fun. 35
   Day One – First Step. 37
      –' I'm Walking in the Snow': 38
       Standing and Getting Moving for the First Time on the Flat. .. 38
      – Moving off on a Slight Gradient Slope and Climbing
       Back to the Start. 38
      – The First Time: This Time on the Lift. 39
      – Stopping. 40
      – Gliding and Variations. 43
   Day One – Second Step. 43
      – Warming-up and Getting Ready. 44
      – The Turn. 44
      – Using the Change of Direction. 48
   Day Two – Third Step. 50
      – Special Swing Movements. 50

INDEX

```
            – Schussing. . . . . . . . . . . . . . . . . . . . . . . . . . . . . . . . . . . . . . . . . .51
            – Body Posture and Using the Board Edges. . . . . . . . . . . . . . . .53
        Day Two – Fourth Step. . . . . . . . . . . . . . . . . . . . . . . . . . . . . . . . . . . . .55
            – Jumping over and Adapting to Small Bumps. . . . . . . . . . . . .56
            – The 'Black Run'. . . . . . . . . . . . . . . . . . . . . . . . . . . . . . . . . . . . .56
            – The Fun-phase. . . . . . . . . . . . . . . . . . . . . . . . . . . . . . . . . . . . .57
        Day Three – Fifth Step. . . . . . . . . . . . . . . . . . . . . . . . . . . . . . . . . . . . .57
            – From BIG FOOT to Skis. . . . . . . . . . . . . . . . . . . . . . . . . . . . . .58
```

6 Playing with the 'Foot' 63

```
    A Collection of Old and New Games on the BIG FOOT . . . . . . . . . . .63
    Games on Flat Snow without Aids . . . . . . . . . . . . . . . . . . . . . . . . . .64
        Relay Races on the Flat. . . . . . . . . . . . . . . . . . . . . . . . . . . . . . . . .64
        Catching and Throwing Games . . . . . . . . . . . . . . . . . . . . . . . . .65
        Dancing on the BIG FOOT . . . . . . . . . . . . . . . . . . . . . . . . . . . . .65
        Gymnastics and Stretching Exercises with BIG FOOT . . . . . . . .67
    Games in the Snow without Aids on the Slope . . . . . . . . . . . . . . . .68
        Relay Races on the Slope . . . . . . . . . . . . . . . . . . . . . . . . . . . . . .68
        Tasks and Playing . . . . . . . . . . . . . . . . . . . . . . . . . . . . . . . . . . . .71
        Playing with the Swing . . . . . . . . . . . . . . . . . . . . . . . . . . . . . . . .72
        Games with the Swing . . . . . . . . . . . . . . . . . . . . . . . . . . . . . . . .73
        Dancing with BIG FOOT . . . . . . . . . . . . . . . . . . . . . . . . . . . . . . .75
        Lots and Lots of BIG FOOT: Building Formations . . . . . . . . . . . .76
    Games on Flat Snow with Aids . . . . . . . . . . . . . . . . . . . . . . . . . . . . .78
    Games in the Snow with Aids on the Slope . . . . . . . . . . . . . . . . . . .78
        Picking up Objects. . . . . . . . . . . . . . . . . . . . . . . . . . . . . . . . . . . .79
        Jumping Games . . . . . . . . . . . . . . . . . . . . . . . . . . . . . . . . . . . . .79
        Games with the Swing, Dancing and Running Blindfold . . . . . .81
        Slalom and Obstacle Courses . . . . . . . . . . . . . . . . . . . . . . . . . . .84
    BIG FOOT Rallying . . . . . . . . . . . . . . . . . . . . . . . . . . . . . . . . . . . . . . .84
```

INDEX

7 'It Does not Always Have To Be Two Metres Long' –
Possibilities for the BIG FOOT Connoisseur 87
  'Step Slope, Moguls, Halfpipes? – And?' 87
  Step Slope 89
  Moguls 91
  Halfpipes and other Snowboarding Territory 93

8 BIG FOOT and 'Classic' Swing Techniques – Incompatible? 97
  The Rotation Technique 98
  Leg Extension Technique 98
  Side-slipping Technique 102

9 With BIG FOOT amongst the Slalom Poles. 105
  Equipment 107
  Course Building 109
  Slalom Skills. 110
  Slalom in Difficult Terrain 111
  Tactics and Techniques 112

10 'Up in the Clouds' –
Flying School for 'Jumpers' with Shoe Size 24 and Larger ...115
  The Upright Jump. 117
  Jumping with a Change of Direction. 118
  Open Leg Jump 118
  The 'Duffy' or Airwalk. 118
  The Knees-bend Jump 118
  Jumping into Voids. 120

11 The Swing à la BIG FOOT – Carving on BIG FOOT 121

12 'Feet Gone to Sleep?' – Carring on BIG FOOT 121
  No Thank You! Getting Used to Skiing with BIG FOOT 127

INDEX

Perceptiveness 129
Body Tension 130
Breathing and Rhythm 132
Application 133

13 'Get into the Rhythm' on 'Large Feet' 135
'Move Your Body !' – Rhythmic Tuning and Warming-up 136
Down the Mountain with a Rhythm 137

14 'Footsteps in the Sand ?' – A Preview 141

15 Literature 142

1 GETTING STARTED

'Short Skis!' That was the initial thought that went through our minds when for the first time, in 1990, we had the BIG FOOT skis under our feet. However straight away, after an hour, we knew we had made a discovery which would certainly enrich our future holidays.

Only after a while did it become crystal clear that these would play such an important role, e.g., for group leaders of skiing holidays with different standards of skiers.

After more than six years of experience with BIG FOOT we felt it very suitable to publish our results. Firstly, there was only rather skimpy documentation on the subject and this was mostly stiff and very theoretical. However, since we found an absolutely positive response on the piste whenever we managed to persuade someone or other to 'sacrifice' one of his valuable skiing days in order to come with us for a BIG FOOT tour, we finally decided, in 1995, to write this book.

In doing so we wanted to contribute towards making this fun machine popular, and to make its diverse advantages clear. It seemed to us that it was important to leave out long-winded and theoretical explanations, which in our opinion are somewhat a contradiction to the equipment itself – in any case the best way to get to know them is by using the old adage:

Strap them on, get some practice in – and simply have fun!

Thus we started our project, and have received friendly support in all of this from a variety of different directions.

In this respect our thanks go the KNEISSL Company, in particular to Dr Spazier who magnanimously placed considerable material at our disposal while we were undertaking the advanced skiing courses with the instructors from CSC Reiseveranstalters (Holiday Organisers, Arnsberg Germany). The photographs, which we have used to illustrate and demonstrate the texts, were shot during this instruction.

A special thanks goes to Professor Gerhard Neisel, Ingeborg Bergmann, Angelika Butz, Michael Epple, Michael Menzel, Renate Scholz and Susanne Wunder. Similarly thanks are due to Simone von Broich who contributed the chapter 'Get into the Rhythm' on BIG FOOT. Additionally a well earned thanks goes to all the 'photo models' who became involved with us, and who, together with BIG FOOT, cut some good figures.

Christian and Stefan

P.S. In our text, we have not differentiated between BIG FOOT girls and BIG FOOT boys. This does not mean that we are expounding some kind of emancipatory backward step – merely we speak of BIG FOOT-runners to help the readability of the book.

2 MENTAL PREPARATION

BIG FOOT:
A Big Deal? – Last Chance?

We do not wish to force BIG FOOT down your throats! – Whether we have found the fount of all knowledge, or discovered the oracle, will be decided by the future BIG FOOT fan, when he has read our deliberately simply worded book and has tried out BIG FOOT-ing afterwards.

Theoretical discussions, full of profound pedagogic build up and different explanations, as well as an attempt to justify what is being written so that even critics would be kept at bay – is not for us! This was clear from the start – we have thus saved ourselves and our readers from this. We have treated the obligatory review of the historical development in the same way, as this only goes to show, yet again, that everything was always there and it is only the baby that has been re-christened.

> **For us it is all about adventure – and adventure now!**
> **We want to show:**
> - that it is simply fun to romp about on BIG FOOT,
> - that BIG FOOT aids learning to ski,
> - that it can offer even the expert new dimensions and challenges, and
> - that it gives pleasure in winter sports at every opportunity in the shortest of time.

Similarity of movement with other types of sport can be applied to this fun machine. One recognises the same movements and actions in ice-skating, roller skating and in-line skating.

Experience and prowess gained in other types of sport, such as these, lead to a safe feeling on BIG FOOT irrespective of age:

BIGFOOT

12

BIGFOOT

- no frustration in the early days,
- less fear of steep slopes or icy stretches, and
- lots of possibilities to try out new things and experiment:

These are the characteristics of BIG FOOT!

In this respect this book can only show the way. Nothing is either 'correct' or 'wrong'! However, there are the expressions 'dangerous' and 'not so dangerous'. For example it is not 'dangerous', like snowboarding, to ski on deep snow off-piste, since it is hardly possible because of the boards themselves. Speed, however, is 'dangerous' when skiing with BIG FOOT. Therefore one's sense of responsibility is brought into question in order not to endanger other people by going too fast or by making a mistake. First of all select 'a lower gear' and gradually build up step by step and the fun with this new sports equipment will last longer, and no-one will get hurt.

The way this book has been put together makes the requirement quite clear that fun and safety in winter sports do not necessarily have to be contradictions in themselves. Once you have been introduced to the handling of the equipment and its possibilities even the layman will quickly recognise that BIG FOOT has several particular advantages over the 'long slats'. Nevertheless we do not wish to convert any skier so that he lets his skis gather dust in the cellar – we also love skiing. As a basic rule there is no such thing as 'either – or'. On the contrary a 'just as much' and an 'as well' turns this into an extension of winter sport pleasure – because, as everyone will find out:

A day on BIG FOOT is not to be counted as a lost day of skiing, even for the professionals.

For many, winter sports mean also family sport or group sport. Thus we show you possibilities of how you can teach children or friends to ski, above all quickly and with a lot of fun. We give suggestions on how to learn new skills. We also take the mystery out of how to get used to a variety of terrain e.g., moguls, or a steep icy slopes which we want you to 'conquer'. A collection of ideas for movement, games and challenging tasks is included as possible ways of setting the programme for a day's outing or ski-course.

We have given you our experiences in short and to the point – without any diversion into the so-called school of knowledge – rather more in a practical way – all you need to do is to observe and try it out. We use the principle that everyone has to gain a certain amount of his own experience before he can learn something and adapt to his own style. This book therefore varies from the conventional concept – we are not about to push you back into school to slave through a teaching programme. Much more we simply want to introduce you to an article of winter sports equipment and the joy it brings with it, and which, BIG FOOT, in our opinion does for every level of ability. You will see that, after trying it out, for most people the following will be true:

Once you have been on BIG FOOT you will certainly be often pulling on these 'big feet'.

3 INTRODUCTION TO THE 'FOOT'

Anatomy

BIG FOOT appears, as the name suggests, just like oversize feet. They are about 24 ins (63 cm) long (i.e., two feet!), broader than conventional alpine skis and have a continuous metal edge. At first sight they seem rather plump, but despite this, when one looks more closely a second time, one discovers a well-formed waist.

On the tips of the BIG FOOT you can see toes clearly marked. The design is very noticeable, and those, who have stood in a lift queue, have heard the remarks "Can you actually ski with those things?", and, "Did you have them on the bath and they have shrunk?" or "Are they really fun?" We are sure you will find a suitable retort to all these comments.

The BIG FOOT does away with the need for a safety binding. The risk of injury in a fall with such short equipment is very small. In the meanwhile three different types of bindings are used. Normal ski boots will fit on all of them. Older models are fitted with a stretch-clip attached to the rear-side of the ski boot which is closed by pushing down on a lever. Amongst other things this action leads to amusing slapstick antics when trying to clip up the second BIG FOOT. With the newer models ('The Brave' and 'Who') there is a rapid-adjustable stretch-clip used, which is mounted in front of the ski boot. Certain models are fitted with a so-called 'step-in' binding. This affords an easy way of clipping into the equipment (see page 20). You will find more on bindings in the next chapter. All skis have a safety ankle binding. This serves not so much towards safety after a fall, as experience will show you that one rarely loses the 'big feet' after an involuntary stunt. They are there more for safety when putting them on or taking them off.

>>**WARNING**: 'Loose' BIG FOOT move with considerable speed downhill – something one would not believe by merely looking at them.<<

BIG FOOT

16

BIG FOOT

The construction of BIG FOOT has remained generally unchanged since they first appeared. The nuances and improvements can be found more in the detail. The first types we tested had a two-piece steel edge. This led to several cases of ending up with firewood through the weakness in the heel region giving way particularly after jumps. Since that time, however, with a continuous steel edge being used, one would really have to be fierce to achieve the same effect. Similarly the plastic heel binding has been subjected to some rapid evolutionary material improvements. The problem with worn teeth in the binding lock has now been banished to the past since the discovery of a metal replacement. Tightening adjustments carried out several times make this binding stronger.

The biggest step towards comfort was, amongst others, the change-over to the front-fitted quick-lock binding arrangement. Not only did this reduce the time taken to clip-up to a minimum, it also avoided the odd breakout of temper. For this and other practical improvements in the equipment, the manufacturers deserve a large pat on the back.

BIGFOOT

18

BIG FOOT

The 1996/97 season saw the introduction of a further new improvement for the BIG FOOT sector with the model 'Trick'. It differs from its predecessors by being about 4 ins (9 cm) longer. Also at the heel is a shovel resembling a foot. Its speciality is principally the halfpipe, where skiing backwards is just as important as skiing forwards. In the meanwhile the 'Trick' has been replaced by the 'BIG FOOT 360'. This has small binding plates which prevent the ski boots coming into contact with the snow while executing extremely tight turns. This feature makes them ideal training equipment for all types of carving. Besides this it keeps pace with general improvements, all models having a front mounted binding.

Handling

With BIG FOOT on the slopes one is nothing special but one has got something special nevertheless.

This already begins with the action of strapping them on. While many alpine skiers often chuck down their skis on the ground haphazardly, step into the bindings and rapidly disappear with a ski-lift, the first step for us BIG FOOT pilots is putting them on. If our 'feet' are the new model types with front rapid-click adjustable bindings all this will be no problem.

If you do not find a lever at the front of the binding then this means you have a model with the older type of binding. Warming-up exercises prior to doing-up the bindings can be beneficial in avoiding stretched muscles. The principles of doing-up the older type of BIG FOOT bindings which offer the best success are as follows:

1. **Lay your BIG FOOT down carefully on the snow so they do not slide away.**
2. Remove all the snow from underneath the ski boots.

BIGFOOT

3. Place your foot into the front binding.
4. Close the rear clip binding.
5. Put the safety binding on round the ankle.

With the new sort of binding the main problems experienced before are happily a thing of the past. If you are doing up your BIG FOOT on a steep slope make sure you follow Point 1 above carefully.

Because they have no brakes BIG FOOT has a habit of shooting off quite happily. If this happens no amount of sprinting after them will help. One can only hope and pray that any damage remains a minimum.

BIGFOOT

Once fixed on and buckled up, however, you can start to enjoy the fun. As experience shows, if there is a stamped label on the bindings, like the old ones, which says 'Not a safety binding' or 'Non quick release', or similar wording, then this is quite OK. Not even an almighty crash-out has caused the binding to release itself yet. This fact, however, should not make you uneasy. By virtue of its short length the risk of injury in a fall with BIG FOOT is extraordinarily low. One thing you can be glad about is, no longer will you be bothered about the annoying necessity of having to gather up the bits and pieces of your equipment after a fall. The motto is 'Fall down – stand-up – carry on skiing'.

The pain of having to pay out so much to buy the equipment in the first place – from about £100 (1998) upwards, can be put into its relativity as follows: The boot adjustable area on older models will accept boot sizes for ladies or children's sizes sole length 9 ins/23 cm (approx. size 3) to the big boot sizes of sole length 15 ins/38 cm (approx. size 12). The adjustable area on the new models is a little less generous but it will still be in the region of 10 ins/25 cm to 14 ins/35 cm. This range of acceptability makes BIG FOOT, therefore, an ideal family piece of equipment. In the morning the children 'live' on them, and in the afternoon the bigger brothers and sisters, or the grown ups have their chance. No other sports equipment possesses this kind of universal versatility. On older models to make the switch to use them from extremely small to large, you must have a medium sized Phillips screwdriver available. This is required to move and adjust the base-plate for the binding.

As a principle BIG FOOT should be used without ski sticks. This is not only to save the bother of having to pick them up after a fall, but mainly because the skiing posture without sticks is deeper and therefore more stable. If they are used they automatically lead one to adopt rather an upright body position. This is, however, not a style to be encouraged. A low body posture affords, as we have said, a better stable ride, and allows one

BIG FOOT

to correct any imperfections easily. We should, however, point out in all honesty, that this correct style of riding BIG FOOT is more exhausting than normal skiing.

BIG FOOT can be carried very easily over the shoulder if one ties the safety bindings together. If you are skiing to the slopes and carrying them, it is recommended that you use a rucksack for them. There are several good ones about – the Austrian Company 'Kneissl' makes a suitable one for instance. However, care must be taken. If you fall with the BIG FOOT in a rucksack the steel edges on them can cause a few big surprises! If you are carrying them like this then you should seek out a suitable system to avoid damage to yourself and others – ski carefully!

Using BIG FOOT on the ski-lift – a subject which for some is a wretched experience – is also conducted without absolutely any problem. Not only do you find that suddenly you have a surprising amount of manoeuvrability in lift queues, you can also have a lot of fun riding up the lift.

Finally, a subject, which is often neglected by many a skier – care and cleaning of the equipment. Just like alpine skis BIG FOOT needs regular servicing. After each day of skiing, the bindings, which are rather susceptible to repair, must be checked over. Damage to them has often been the cause of many an unexpected fall. Similarly the surface should be rubbed down with wax at regular intervals.

Particular care must be taken of the steel edges. Since the main weight is taken by a relatively short length (in comparison to alpine skis) of the edge when riding on them, they naturally tend to be the first thing to show wear. Smoothing the edges by filing them and polishing them when necessary should therefore not be forgotten from time to time. Your BIG FOOT will reward you for the good servicing given, by affording you a lot of fun on the slope and of course – longevity.

Characteristics and Types of Use

One outstanding characteristic of BIG FOOT is its ability to turn so well. Even beginners can quickly learn to enjoy the fun of doing the short turn right from the start. The experienced skier rapidly feels as if he is the king of the slope, and for the connoisseur, opportunities open up for new areas to try, which he might never have found on alpine skis. Any previous experience on roller-, ice-skates, or in-line skates for example, saves the newcomer often long-winded explanations on how to use this equipment. After a short briefing and only a few shaky attempts the fun can usually start straight away.

The search for the best riding position is a little more difficult. A position, leaning too far forward or too far backwards, guarantees a cooling-off in the cold snow. The rather short supporting surfaces in the front and back do not allow for any mistakes. The principle of trial and error, however, soon leads to a 'healthy' central position. If you diverge from this the equipment will soon let you know with a strong fluttering of the 'toes'. Leaning forward removes these symptoms.

Turning on the BIG FOOT can be carried out by using all the usual mechanisms known in skiing. There is no end to all the possibilities open to do this.

BIG FOOT's extremely narrow central waist naturally plays a large role in the skiing style. On a piste which grips well the equipment pulls you into a swing with truly formidable force. Steering with both legs helps to counter the forces created. One can also break-off the swing and transfer into a new swing or even brake. Skiing with BIG FOOT in this manner is covered in Chapter 11, which is entitled 'The Swing à la BIG FOOT'.

BIG FOOT skis are not terribly suitable for skiing in powdery deep snow. Because of their short length they simply do not gather enough lift to keep on the snow surface all the time. Just for fun, and even if only to appreciate their behaviour in a fall, it is worthwhile for everyone to take a spin in deep snow.

Another type of situation, for which BIG FOOT is not suitable, is slushy conditions in Spring. The danger of sticking the 'shovel-shaped' front tips of the skis deep into the surface, and experiencing the unavoidable belly-flop as a consequence, is very high.

Nevertheless experienced 'BIG FOOT-ers' can master such conditions. They use a method, which for most normally leads to landing on your back, namely the switch of the centre of balance towards the heels. If this is done carefully and gently, so that the weight is centred over the rear third of the equipment, then it is possible to glide down the slope rather similar to water-skiing. However the same principle applies to leaning back too far which will lead to a compulsory lie in the snow.

The picture is quite different on a hard slope covered partially by ice – a condition hated by most skiers. For many alpine skiers control of the skis is very difficult because of the limited grip afforded by the side runners of the skis. For BIG FOOT fans, however, the world is totally different and better. Not that the sheets of ice will suddenly become less slippery. Control is still achieved, nevertheless, because of factors such as the main pressure of the side runners being maintained over a shorter length, as well as the simplicity of being able to turn and the lower centre of gravity. Speed remains a problem in these conditions. Therefore always watch your speed on hard and icy slopes, and keep it at a controllable rate at all times so as not to endanger yourself and others. Naturally this particularly applies not only at all times, but also for any ski equipment and slope conditions. The energy required to carry out a braking swing at high speed is considerably higher than required on normal alpine skis. BIG FOOT are particularly more suitable, in principle, to allow the more inexperienced skier to cope with these conditions. The main requirement for skiing with BIG FOOT on very hard surfaces is to keep the side runners sharp and honed.

How you can cope with other difficult types of terrain, such as steep drops and moguls, comes in a later chapter (see page 91 et seq.).

Another usage for BIG FOOT is for touring. They are easily packed into a rucksack and used by expert mountain walkers in powdery snow. By virtue of the construction of the bindings, BIG FOOT can even be strapped underneath climbing boots. However, the boots must be ones which have protruding soles at the tips and the heels over which the bindings can be strapped.

As you can see, BIG FOOT is a very universally adaptable fun machine. We can only recommend that you take a dip into this adventure and try out all the possibilities that they offer. If they fail to please, you will not exactly get your money back – this is a risk. However, according to our experiences, the risk is hardly at any odds and well worth taking.

4 BIG FOOT – FUN FOR THE CHILDREN (AND NOT ONLY THEM)

BIG FOOT has hardly any match as a suitable piece of winter sports equipment to spend happy hours learning on. Their appearance alone exude a pleasing character, full of challenge, for children and grown-ups alike. The way they run on the snow make them popular equipment for beginners. This characteristic ensures that they are fast becoming a firm facet of the beginner's ski school. Suggestions on how you as parents can get your children on their 'feet', or how to get friends and acquaintances to turn their hand to become assistant ski instructors, and get pleasure out of winter sports is described in the following pages. Above all, for children wishing to ski, BIG FOOT can get a lot moving quickly.

**Winter Sports with the Offspring:
How Do I Turn My Children into 'Slippery Slopers'?**

If you decide to accompany and look after your children in their first steps of winter sports and skiing, and do not want to hand over the responsibility to a ski school, then there will be a lot of questions tumbling around in your head.

- How old should the children be before they start?
- What sort of terrain is best for the beginner?
- What do I do to give my child the most fun in winter sports?

We want to try to give you some plausible answers to most of your questions.

In answer to the question regarding age for beginners we quote the German Ski Programme. The first contact with snow, within limitations, is fine for children as young as two years old. The fact that this will not be in

BIGFOOT

the context of ski instruction will be obvious. It should, therefore, be more about letting the children collect basic experience in a new environment. The optimum age to start learning alpine skiing is between 5-10 years old. There is no rule regarding the actual age a start is made by the child. A 10-year old beginner can easily go on to become a very good skier (or 'BIG FOOT-er').

A word about clothing. Always dress your children up in the same manner as you yourself would do for the prevailing weather conditions. A few items to change into in bad weather will always come in useful. Snow-goggles or sun-glasses, as well as sun cream, with an adequate protective factor, are absolute essentials. The light protection factor can never be too high.

Good so far! Now we can really get down to things:

With you holding your child's hands, the first steps and sliding attempts should serve as a happy and child-friendly introduction to this sport. Since the 1997/98 season the Kneissl Company has especially opened its heart to children.

The new models are called BIG FOOT 'Little' and are suitable and safe for even the smallest of boot sizes. Once you see these cute little models it will be love at first sight. Since they are somewhat shorter than normal BIG FOOT (23 $\frac{1}{4}$ ins/59 cm), the smallest of children will be able to have a lot of fun on them. This will have little effect on the skiing manoeuvrability. At such an age one is not talking of free 'schussing' or the like, so it does not really matter. The cost of BIG FOOT 'Little' – at about £35 – keeps the expense within reasonable limits.

The first attempts at moving on the snow should take place on a level surface. This is the best way for your little-ones to get used to the new environment and conditions.

As soon as the child has gained a little confidence in the 'skiworld', it will soon enough want to ski by itself. The first gliding movements should always end, after a few metres, with you safely catching the child. If the child wants to go on further, providing the snow is soft enough, you can always lengthen this distance. In order to allow yourself more manoeuvrability you can follow along these first exercises without having your BIG FOOT (or skis) on. For the transition to individual and independent longer distance 'schuss' exercises (10-20 metres), the most important thing is to choose the right surface. A flat run-out or a lightly rising snow slope is essential.

During this phase you must continually watch the mood and motivation of your child. If it shows no more interest, and words from you fail to motivate any longer, you should stop and try again, perhaps after a pause, or even leave it to start afresh on the next day. Sometimes it is worth employing children's games, like those they make up themselves, as a digression. Examples are:

- Using one of the BIG FOOT as a sledge
- Sliding down on the bottom or on the stomach
- Trying to skate with the ski boots
- Snowball fights
- Using one of the BIG FOOT as a skate-board
- Digging yourself into the snow

In this introductory phase wrongly applied over-zealousness by the parents can result in spoiling the fun. Without fun, learning turns into a drudge. Therefore – always take it slowly.

To reach the schussing phase with a 2-3 year old, where children only imagine one thing, namely to be able to belt down the slope all the time – will perhaps take up the whole of a holiday. For older children, the enthusiasm to try more grows after usually 2-5 days. In order to make the first independent 'runs' interesting, and to bring in variety, one can use numerous little games. Here are a few suggestions:

- Holding a ski stick

- Skiing through gates

- Skiing between Mummy's or Daddy's legs

- Skiing – as small as a mouse
- Skiing – as tall as a giant
- Skiing and picking up objects (gloves, snowballs, soft toys)

If there is a nursery slope in your ski resort of course the next step is to go up the ski-lift with your little-ones. You can prepare for this by pulling the child with a ski stick, which the child holds with both hands – or better still, like a T-bar lift – the child holds onto the ski stick, stuck between your legs. At the beginning you will have to lend some parental help before the child can use the lift properly. This takes the form of having the child between your legs leaning on your shins. Right from the start make sure that your child's weight is standing on his own BIG FOOTs.

For those childminders who are themselves not quite so sure on skis, BIG FOOT are a useful aid to making it simple.

After the schuss there is the question of changing direction. How can you get your child to be able to change direction for the first time? Of course it will not take the form of a lengthy explanation about weight transfers and lifting the foot – or even by you demonstrating it, like in a school programme. The solution lies in using incentives. Using ski sticks, mark out two gates slightly offset from each other on the slope, and encourage your child to ski through them both. After two or three attempts it is certain that you will have some success. You will find that the child will be able to assimilate this without complicated descriptions. The child's technique matters little at this stage.

Success is the important point – not forgetting parental praise. If you have brought your child on so far, then the programme for the following skiing days is set – belting up and down the slope over again and again. However, it is still important that there is some form of variety. You must make sure that lessons already learned are gone over again from time to time. Schussing, skiing holding a steadying hand and being pulled by the ski stick, as well as the games, should often be reintroduced. Variations of the game with ski gate slaloms can make practice for change of direction a fun thing for the children over a longer period e.g.

- Negotiating one gate
- Negotiating two gates
- Build slaloms with several offset gates
- Changing the form and distance between gates
- Inventing games involving stories about going through the gates
- Making the offset differences of the gates greater etc.

Following on from the so-called compulsory changes of direction by virtue of having the gates in front of one, is the ability and important step of being able to change direction at will. As soon as the child sees no gate in front of it there is suddenly no incentive to have to turn. The fact that ski turns are not only used to negotiate gates, but can be used to control the speed, has not yet been realised by the child. This means that you have to ensure that there is sufficient motivation available to the child to learn this. This can be achieved by skiing ahead and playing 'catch' for example, or using some other form of incentive. Other ways could be to note particular landmarks on the side of the piste (certain trees, piste markers, mummy or daddy standing there and so on). Changing places so that you play the child's part, and vice versa, can also work wonders. Let your child lead and play the 'instructor' as it leads you safely down the slope.

Make sure that during all these exercises you are able to help the child at any time. It is possible, even on the nursery slope, that the child can lose control. If a helping hand is not immediately available, depending on the circumstances, it might take a lot of effort and persuasion to negotiate the next slope.

If, finally, your child is able to manage turns and sudden stops on a beginner's slope, then tremendous progress has been made. The main thing is, however, that it is all still fun. After a week it is always better to return to having fun sledging about on the BIG FOOT than to be standing there trying to negotiate a slalom gate with tears in the eyes behind the goggles.

5 IN THE BEGINNING THERE WAS THE FOOT – THE ALTERNATIVE BEGINNER'S COURSE

A 'Recipe' for Fun

We all know the problem where someone in your circle of acquaintances does not like the idea of skiing much, and as a result a holiday together between Christmas and Easter goes out of the window. To whet the beginner's appetite, and to allow him to experience success in no time at all, we will show you a way in which one can learn to ski simply and have fun at the same time. The method is equally suitable for use in putting a beginner's course together, as well as for the self-learners i.e., those who prefer to do away with 'demonstrators of the art' and assimilate skiing on their own. We have gained a lot of experience with our 'recipe' in several beginner's courses. The method contains no lengthy theoretical explanations and no educational descriptions. One should convince oneself by trying it out in practice. Variations, improvements and individual adaptations can be and should be used – everyone learns at a different pace of course. An aid to this can be seen in the next chapter covering the collection of games.

We believe that it is important to develop a solid basis, a guideline so to speak, to which one can attach oneself. We will try to give you a lead on this in this chapter so that you can learn the basics of skiing in a simple and pleasant way.

The method used is that firstly we try out the equipment and have a little trial to get used to skiing along on it. In this way experience is collected which also makes one keen to discover more. Here it is not a question of trying to copy some demonstration, but rather more 'learning by doing'. One quickly gets a feeling for what is going on under the 'BIG FOOT'. Everyone will soon learn to find his own solutions to master the beginner's problems, either spontaneously or little by little, and have fun at the same time without having to put a lot of effort and thought into the process. Another thing to note is that BIG FOOT beginner's courses allow a larger group to take part. There is no waiting about because someone has come out of his bindings, and everyone has to wait while they are strapped on again.

BIGFOOT

BIGFOOT

Day One – First Step:

> The first step takes 2 ½ hours.
> **Aim:** Getting used to moving about normally on BIG FOOT including gliding downhill, climbing back up the slope and braking.
>
> **Terrain:** On the flat to start with, then on a blue piste.

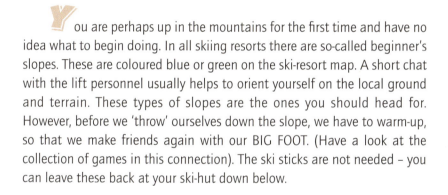

You are perhaps up in the mountains for the first time and have no idea what to begin doing. In all skiing resorts there are so-called beginner's slopes. These are coloured blue or green on the ski-resort map. A short chat with the lift personnel usually helps to orient yourself on the local ground and terrain. These types of slopes are the ones you should head for. However, before we 'throw' ourselves down the slope, we have to warm-up, so that we make friends again with our BIG FOOT. (Have a look at the collection of games in this connection). The ski sticks are not needed – you can leave these back at your ski-hut down below.

When you are strapping on your BIG FOOT you must make sure, above all, that the safety bindings are done up securely. One of these BIG FOOT can be extremely dangerous for the other skiers, even on a piste two or three further down. Anyway, we will get round to skiing on one BIG FOOT later on.

'I'm Walking in the Snow': Standing and Getting Moving for the First Time on the Flat

Try moving, at will, forwards, sideways or backwards. Variations on this are walking, sliding or slipping, and eventually combining this with a half or complete turn. The skating movement is another way, where you push opposite legs forward in turn, just like skating or roller-skating.

Use all the variations. A relay game, or a game using two marked out courts with a tennis ball, handkerchiefs, and so on, is ideal for improving your feeling for BIG FOOT.

Moving off on a Slight Gradient Slope and Climbing Back to the Start

No matter which way you turn or twist, there will always be two ways: Either you climb up the slope and ski down it or vice versa. The exhausting climb up is unavoidable, and this has to be done in a particular way so that you do not end up going backwards downhill instead of uphill. NB., one edge of the BIG FOOT must always be dug into the slope (called 'edging'). Since we have not practised braking yet, there is one thing we would urge – do not climb up too far or ski down too far, and above all do not attempt your first downhill runs on steep slopes.

The two ways used to climb up the piste are the herring-bone (on the right) and the side-stepping methods (on the left). The obviousness of their names, and the distinct pattern they leave in the snow, make any further explanation somewhat superfluous.

The First Time: This Time on the Lift

Well, that's enough climbing for now! As soon as you feel confident enough it is time to try the lift. There are chair lifts or tow lifts ('T-bar' and 'Poma' lifts). Let's look at the tow lifts. But how do we use them? It is quite important that you do not try and sit on the cross-bar, because after all it is not a chair lift. Just stand relaxed with the inside hand on the supporting pole. Your BIG FOOT should be placed on the ground, shoulder width apart and parallel to each other. Off we go!

However, it is possible of course to slip out of the cross-bar. This will happen to everyone at least once. It is then important to clear the path as quickly as possible. Watchful lift attendants will normally stop the lift for a short pause to allow you to sort yourself out. When you are carrying out a normal exit from the lift at the proper exit point make sure you move off in the signed direction to lead you off the path. Help from an experienced skier accompanying you will always be welcomed.

So that you can experience what the lift feels like prior to your first time, two of your group, holding onto a ski stick, can pull a third person along uphill. Simultaneously the 'pullers' can practise their climbing and edging skills.

Stopping

Yes – let's now turn to the most important point. As a good BIG FOOT skier, or as just simply an alpine skier, one must be able to stop in any circumstance.

You should not ski too fast, because otherwise you cannot guarantee that you will be able to stop at any given moment. Indeed, in an emergency there is always the reliable braking method which we call the 'textile brake'. In other words, whenever there is no other alternative, you can fall over i.e., throw yourself down into the snow in a controlled manner, but watch how you do this.

How do I learn to stop?

Try learning by doing. Just ski down the slope and try to stop as quickly as possible. For safety reasons you should never ski towards

BIGFOOT

another skier, and you should always stand downhill from individuals or a group of people. Very often you can misjudge the distance and you do not stop in time. Therefore start slowly and gradually improve your braking. Of course, a better method than the so-called 'textile brake' is the snow plough. Bring the two big thick 'toes' together at the tips and push or spread the rear ends of the BIG FOOT wide. Another braking possibility is simply to try to ski round in a curve and back uphill.

Besides these methods another suitable one is the skid turn leading to a halt – sometimes called 'Braquage'. Both of your BIG FOOT are brought parallel to each other by bending and unweighting, and eventually placed across your skiing line in a skid – similar to ice-skating. Try out the various methods until you find which is the most effective.

Start with the snow plough and move on later to the skid turn stop (braquage). The latter is more dynamic, dependant on the effort placed into the bending and unweighting movement applied. Further exercises, using all the methods in turn and with the aim of testing which method is the best, are as follows:

- Ski down and stop as soon as possible having passed a pre-determined spot (marked in the snow).
- Ski down and stop exactly at a predetermined spot.

You can get a better idea of the advantages of each method if you do this in a group with each member trying out a different stop system. One way of improving your braking is to play the game 'grandma's footsteps' (see 'Selection of Games' in the next chapter).

BIGFOOT

42

Gliding and Variations

Once we can brake well you should begin to try out the various ski gliding methods in order to improve this facet. This will help to improve your balance in tricky situations. Just try out various different ways of skiing. Use your own fantasy – whether it be to go backwards, sideways, standing on one leg or twisting about the axis – just about any way goes.

Day One - Second Step

The second step takes 2-3 hours.

Aims: Exercise to try out the various possibilities of changing direction on BIG FOOT – carried out on a 'red run' at a controlled average pace – using one or other of the methods learnt already – as well as coming safely to a halt.

Terrain: First on a 'blue run' moving later to an easy 'red run'.

BIGFOOT

Warming-up and Getting Ready

▶ The progress that you have made during the beginning phase of your learning should be revised and firmed up in the afternoon. At this time it is very easy to overestimate your own ability, so it is important to keep your speed down. Take the afternoon revision at a suitably reduced speed. Prior to doing this you should carry out an effective warming-up programme of exercises.

Practise your skiing thoroughly on a flat area. Following this try to get the feeling of the BIG FOOT well into your mind and warm-up without setting yourself any particular tasks e.g., do a couple of runs down the 'blue run' with a pause in between. Then afterwards you can try the first part of turning – without ski sticks.

The Turn

▶ The turn is a basic skill – equal in importance to stopping. Alpine skiers speak of 'flowing like a river'.

This expression says it all. The main system of learning the turn is to try and create 'as twisty a river as possible' as you ski, traversing, down the slope.

During your exercises watch out that you obey the 'right of way' rules. Before you move off, this means: look up the slope to see if the way is clear. If you are underway the rule is that whoever is coming down must give way to the skier lower down. On the contrary the skier lower down need not look back up the slope as soon as he hears the scrape of ski edges. However, overcautiousness can lead to mistakes.

Let's get back to the turn:
There are different ways to execute the turn. As a general principle you should try to keep your knees bent and forward and also slightly lean forward from the hips. In our course we list the most common solutions below. The best way, as always, is simply to try out all the possibilities at least once.

Using Your Head – Literally

Aha! Craning your neck to follow that nice looking young man or girl? – This is the phenomenon of the mirage in the desert! Far and wide only a palm tree and I drive my vehicle relentlessly towards it. Why? Keeping it in sight is all that is required. Well, it is the same with changing direction – the turn. If you turn your head alternately to one side – left or right – for long enough, you will go in that direction. By the way, this is not a method you should try out on a busy piste!

Skiing – the Ice-Block Way

Tense all your muscles – first your legs and then your bottom. Follow this by tensing the stomach muscles, and finally the arms down to your fists. You now resemble a block of 'ice' – totally formidable and rigid. By maintaining the tension you will be able to ski in smooth curves and turns.

A Small Step – Large Effect

While skiing down the fall line push the downhill leg forward – or better still lift it a little. As you do this your opposite arm swings forward – just like walking. As an example let's repeat that – so; right leg forward and left arm forward – and hey presto you are already making a lovely right turn. Left leg forward and right arm forward and you're turning left. Why is this? By lifting one of the BIG FOOT, automatically there is stronger pressure on the other one; the outside BIG FOOT takes all the weight and takes up the steering by using the effect of the counter balance of the arm outstretched and forward.

Top Tip: Leave the arm outstretched and forward right up until the completion of the turn.

Rotating – but not too Far

You turn your upper body in a different direction. You can induce the swing by bending and pulling your arm, stretched out horizontally into the body. As it blocks against the body suddenly, your legs follow a fraction of a second later and you turn in the direction of the swing. The rotation should not go too far – e.g., so far that you cannot see behind or further up the slope. Also not too far if you hear the scraping sounds of a skier on the slope to your uphill side (see the 'right of way rules' earlier).

Turning the Legs

This is simple on BIG FOOT. And it does not take as long to master as it does on normal skis. Hold your upper body still or turn it at the beginning as an aid to counterbalance your legs. Try to turn your legs (i.e., the parts below the knee – the lower leg, shins and feet) in a different direction. A change of direction will occur seemingly automatically if you press, for a quick instant, the inside edge of the BIG FOOT into the snow. At the same time you must press your knees into the slope according to which side your turn is directed. To check whether you are really actually turning by using your legs, lay your hands on your knees and hold your upper body still. Now do your turns so that they are being steered actually by the lower legs.

The Up and Down Movement

This goes back to an old tradition, and was once very important to skiers. It transmits a dynamic feeling. The up and down movement is very often a valuable aid for beginners. You are skiing across the slope stooped

BIG FOOT

down in a low posture. Your knees are slightly forward and pressed into the slope. The upper body and hips are also leaning slightly forward and turned into the slope. By dynamically stretching the legs you turn and change direction. On completion you return to your starting posture. You can vary this; if you stay stretched 'up' longer and then return slowly to the 'down' posture then the turn will be a long curve. The quicker you carry out the movements the sharper the turns become. With an explosive 'up' movement you will even be able to jump into a change of direction. You can support the 'up' movement with the arms.

Using the Change of Direction

The ways to effect a turn that we have described above all stem from 'discoveries' made by participants on our courses. Of course you will have similar experiences and 'discoveries' when you trace out 'the twisty flowing river' in the snow. So that you can try out different solutions, and can recognise which technique is the best to match to which set of circumstances, here are some suggestions for your training periods.

1) **Turning in a Funnel Formed by Ski Poles**
   Place ski poles into the snow so that they form a funnel. The ones higher up should be placed generously apart – up to 8 m. As one comes down the funnel the distance between them is made smaller until they are 1 m apart. On the fall line the poles should be about 2 m apart. Now try to ski across the 'funnel' from one pole to the opposite one. The radii of your turns will automatically become smaller.

2) **The Slalom**
   A slalom through ski poles automatically forces you to make certain turns since the idea is to ski in and out of them. This exercise will soon give you a measure of how far you have progressed with your turn.

3) **High Speed Turns and Steep Slopes**
   Just as with other training steps, it is equally true that when you can carry out the phases well and without effort, you are then ready to face further challenges such as a higher speed and more difficult terrain. Thus you can now increase your skiing-speed a little and do your turns correctly on a 'blue run'. If this goes well the next challenge will be to try some slow turns on a more steeply sloping terrain ('red run').

4) **'Follow My Leader'**
   A special use for the turn is skiing while playing 'follow my leader'. Everyone follows the lead skier, who should set the pace such that everyone can follow. Each skier will be so concentrating on keeping on the path and following that there will be little time to notice anything else. This serves as a good learning practice.

5) **Partner Skiing**
   Both partners hold their ski poles horizontally in front of them. Now ski down the slope next to each other using differently sized radii for each turn. The outside partner will always have a longer distance to cover than the inside skier. This means that each one will have to adapt continually to changing circumstances.

Downhill

As a general rule you will be able to master a downhill run, accompanied by good skiers, on the first day out, as long as the downhill is not any more difficult than a 'red run'. Therefore you should save some energy for this and programme some time for it. There is perhaps no better a morale lifting experience than to be able to ski all the way down to the bottom of the run on your first day. You get a feeling of achievement "I can already do it !", and you think to yourself "Tomorrow I will manage more!"

Day Two – Third Step

> The third step – a new day dawns – more fun – takes another two hours.
>
> **Aims:** Deliberately try out the various possibilities of changing direction on a variety of different grades of difficult terrain; increase speed.
>
> **Terrain:** First on an easy 'red run', moving later to more difficult 'red runs'.

Rested, you begin your new day, as always, with a period of warming-up exercises. You will find some suggestions in the collection of games. You will also notice other skiing groups carrying out their warming-up exercises, and it is quite possible you can borrow some of their ideas. Afterwards you should get your eye in by doing a ski run which can serve also to introduce you to a new run.

Special Swing Movements

In order to deepen your expertise in the various possibilities of carrying out the turn, it is a good idea to try out the different special swing movements contained in the selection of games (see the detailed explanation of these movements in the section 'Playing with the Foot'). The games are laid out in a special order so that the turns progress from ones with a large radius to ones with a small radius.

You should start with the 'Boxer' swing, follow on with the 'Marmot' swing before moving on and up into the clouds with the 'Eagle' swing. Then finally try out the 'The Aeroplane' swing. All of these swing movements depend on a different basic principle to trigger off the turn. Try and discover what these principles are. You will soon latch onto the secret of the principles if you try them all out individually in turn.

Schussing

Exercise: ski about 20 metres down the fall line and come to a halt standing upright. This exercise carries a small risk of course. Everyone learns to judge his own actions. Be careful and make sure that the slope is not too steep. There is no mysticism about speed – one can learn to master it. Start slowly with a safe posture, and then you are off – faster and faster....

You can adopt a number of different postures. You can alter your stoop – sometimes low down and sometimes more upright. The same applies to the distance between your BIG FOOT – narrowly apart, a hip's width apart or even wider. Try out various ways and make a note – when do you pick up speed, when do you feel most comfortable and safe?

A 'schuss' a day keeps the boredom at bay!

Skis placed a hip's width apart, the elbows pressed into the front of the kneecaps and your forearms held horizontally – this is what constitutes a safe posture.

The next exercise: carry out a schuss and keep pushing one leg in front of the other alternately as you ski down. Using this method you are now learning a further way to conduct a turn. The centre of balance automatically changes as each of your BIG FOOT takes up more pressure. This effect will be more pronounced when the edge of the trailing BIG FOOT is dug in deeper. Thus we move onto the next major point – getting the feel for 'edging'. But before we do, here is an important tip. Once you

BIGFOOT

are in a schuss position and get the feeling you are going too fast, maintain your posture. If you 'open up' i.e., change your posture and adopt a more upright position the pressure of the wind will push you over backwards and you will crash out.

A crash like this constitutes the most dangerous thing for a BIG FOOTer. Obey the rule therefore: slow down your speed by turning into the slope (turn uphill).

Body Posture and Using the Board Edges

When the lowland Tiroleans start to come to grips with their mountains and snow, there are a few things that even they need some time before they become intuitively drilled into them, unlike the experienced mountain people, for whom these things come as naturally inborn. If, up to now we have avoided the theory somewhat, then we reach a point when, without trying to underline the fact, we will only be able to progress haltingly with the little experience that we have gained so far. A short dissertation on the most important of the biomechanical principles which you can try out will broaden our spectrum of the steps and manner of conducting ourselves. Anyway – and this is a good reason to make the effort – the exercises will increase the safety factor.

Each pressure point in the foot has a particular correlation with a specific posture of the body, and thus has a bearing on your posture on the BIG FOOT. To find out what these are practise the following exercises:

- Ski down a relatively simple downhill section of the red run and shift your weight first onto one of your BIG FOOT and then onto the other.
- Concentrate on your right foot and change the pressure along the whole length of the BIG FOOT, from the inside edge into the middle and then to the outside edge.
- Do the same exercise but this time with both feet simultaneously.

BIGFOOT

The most important thing with this exercise is to realise how your knees change position and what effect the changes make. Pressure on the inside edge of the foot means: the knee pushes into the inside and the BIG FOOT is slanted inwards. If this is done underway it means that you will execute a curve turn called 'carving'. The degree of the curve turn will sharpen if you simultaneously press down on the outside edge of the other foot as well.

Other parts of the body to which pressure can be applied, and which play a part in determining different body positions, are the shins and calves. In general one rides on BIG FOOT in the upright position. Leaning backwards too much has only one result – you will end up on your back. Leaning forwards too much results in the 'big toe' digging in and similarly you will be soon applying the 'textile' brake.

The next exercise: take up a position on BIG FOOT so that you can feel that your calves are pressing down. Next, ski so that you feel pressure on your shins. At the same time 'sink' down into your ski boots. In this exercise it is important that you take the trouble to ensure that you actually feel the different pressure points that can be applied, merely by changing the position of the knees.

You will notice that you can ski the safest and surest by using pressure on the shins. BIG FOOT do not wobble about their axis when one is skiing normally. Wobbling is very often noticeable even with good skiers when they try out BIG FOOT for the first time.

Okay – that's enough theory. The following exercise serves to increase safety on the piste. Ski across the slope, and without slipping, first of all to the right side and then to the left side (to exercise both legs). Notice the pressure points you are using in each of the positions you adopt in order to successfully carry out the exercise.

The last exercise in this series serves to strengthen your feel for the edging movement. Slide sideways down the slope and carry out a short edging of both BIG FOOT skis into the side of the slope. (Downhill – BIG FOOT – inside edge; uphill – BIG FOOT – outside edge.) Using this method you will be able to master even the difficult parts of the piste later on.

To finish off before your lunch break you should go through all you have learned once again. A suggestion is to do it in pairs – shadowing each other and scribing different radii – this means that you have to alternately apply pressure, sometimes for a lengthy period, sometimes just for short periods. Shadowing teaches you also good reaction and above all is a lot of fun.

Day Two - Fourth Step

The fourth step – and another 2 $\frac{1}{2}$ hours.

Aim: Controlled skiing in difficult terrain using hillocks (bumps) to perform the jump.

Terrain: Difficult 'red runs' with little hillocks, moving later to an 'easy' black run without hillocks.

Terrain is one of the handicaps over which you have no influence. Find out what you can do with your BIG FOOT in different types of terrain.

Jumping over and Adapting to Small Bumps

You will slowly progress from differing bumpy ground and get used to difficult terrain. With this come the first attempts at jumping. Your reaction and adaptability will be improved using this approach. Negotiating bumps plays an important role in skiing on uneven ground.

An essential prerequisite is good body tension. So tighten up the muscles in your stomach, arms, legs and buttocks and try first of all to jump over a small obstacle.

Second exercise: try to ski over a bump without your BIG FOOT losing contact with the snow (compensate and bend). The motto is 'keep your feet on the ground' i.e., keep your legs relaxed and do not lift off the ground.

Finally – try to be catapulted into the air by using the bump. Watch your speed. Remember – start slowly and gradually increase the tempo. If you want to you can use the bump also to change direction. On landing, besides keeping your balance, you must flex your legs to soften the touchdown.

Once you ski off home at the end you can use all the teaching and experience to go over all the uneven spots you meet on the ground in a variety of ways.

The 'Black Run'

One cannot simply 'black-out' the day that one first went down the black run – the memory will remain with you forever. A 'black run' is a very special experience. It is better to do it with a number of people together, some even experts. This will ensure it does not become one of your 'black days' in your career as a budding BIG FOOTer. You will soon find out that doing a 'black run' is all about hard work – and more hard work – and more hard work... And that's where we begin.

An improvement in your assimilated abilities can only be achieved when you set your sights high i.e., when you are prepared to accept all the challenges. Edging exercises and traversing should be repeated for practice – also changing direction, which should be carried out on this kind of run at a speed as slow as possible to start with.

You must check out all the experiences you have made to date and go through the exercises conscientiously. If you have managed to master the 'black run' – with or perhaps even without scaring the living daylights out of yourself – then the door is open for you to conquer the whole of the ski region in the future.

The Fun-phase

So that you can end the day pleasantly after all the drudgery, the rest of the day should be spent having some fun on your BIG FOOT. Item 1 on your menu of things to do should include your own selection of exercises such as 'follow my leader', the waltz, doing pirouettes, jumping and funny turns. Of course you can make up some new ideas yourself and try them out (see our collection of games later).

Day Three – Fifth Step

The fifth step
From BIG FOOT onto the 'long planks'
Aim: Controlled skiing and turning together with skiers.
Terrain: First of all on a simple 'blue run' and then finally on an 'easy' red run.

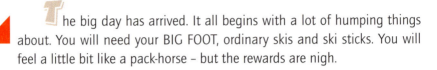

From BIG FOOT to Skis

The big day has arrived. It all begins with a lot of humping things about. You will need your BIG FOOT, ordinary skis and ski sticks. You will feel a little bit like a pack-horse – but the rewards are nigh.

The first two days were coupled with fun. Before we 'pack it (the fun) in', because we are going to get really serious, just let's have a little more. Warm-up on a 'blue run' with your BIG FOOT and take your ski sticks with you, because in future they will always be your companion.

Leave your skis for the moment somewhere near the 'blue run', which, where possible, should be the same run that you used on Day 1. Once you have warmed-up you can now get on with **the first big important step – skiing with one BIG FOOT and one ski at the same time.**

In order to ascertain the difference between BIG FOOT and skis you must have a simple comparison. Strap a ski on your 'strongest' foot and put your BIG FOOT on the other. Before strapping on the ski get some tips and an explanation of the ski binding from a competent skier nearby.

Now try to ski off in a couple of curves or so without your ski sticks and get the feeling of the difference between the way the two react. You will notice very quickly that you have to work more with the foot that has the ski. You will have to edge deeper, carry out more compensating up and down movements with the legs, switch your weight more often or simply have to allow more time to ski round a curve – these are all new experiences that you will have to adjust to on the 'long planks'.

After the first few trial runs you should bring the ski sticks into the equation. After you have tried this all out for some time, it is not only possible but also makes sense to swap over BIG FOOT and skis onto the

BIG FOOT

other feet. During the whole of this phase you must try to remember the exercises that you carried out on BIG FOOT in your first two days. Try them all out again, one after the other, but this time with one BIG FOOT and one ski on.

Going around and skiing with one BIG FOOT and one ski is no easy exercise – even for advanced students.

Exercises to be mastered with the one BIG FOOT/one ski combination are as follows:
- Skiing in different positions (schussing, leaning forward and leaning backwards)
- Braking
- Edging while traversing
- Side-slipping and edging
- Skiing downhill changing weight by taking a step, and later by unweighting one foot after the other (weight transfer).

You will soon realise that the odd feeling of one item being much longer than the other disappears after about half-an-hour and you are soon able to do ski turns quickly again. After you have completed all the exercises with the one BIG FOOT/one ski combination you can decide for yourself if and when you strap on both skis and hang your BIG FOOT up on the nail for a while. An advantage of the BIG FOOT is that you can decide for yourself when the right moment is to change over to skis. The group, despite differing ability, can ski together whether it is with the one BIG FOOT/one ski combination or with skis alone. By choosing the popular carving skis, now available on the market, these allow you to venture directly from BIG FOOT onto two skis. We recommend you use the relatively shorter carving model (approx 60-65 inches (150-160 cm) long).

BIGFOOT

Further progress on skis rather depends on you. Perhaps it is recommended at this point that you take part on a ski course. You will find a lot of similarities in the exercises that you know from BIG FOOT. What you will avoid is the frustration that often accompanies learning to ski without the relaxing enjoyable preparatory work.

Oh yes – and in the afternoon you should stop and have a rest and let your body relax. This will ensure that you end the fourth day fit enough to strap on two skis. Also you should be aware that, according to statistics, most of the ski accidents happen on Day 3!

BIGFOOT

62

6 PLAYING WITH THE 'FOOT'
A Collection of Old and New Games on the BIG FOOT

In this section we have illustrated some games that can be used in differing situations. Each game is aimed at a particular group and has a different set of aims. The selection shown is aimed at encouraging further development or variation of the game, or to spark off ideas for new games. Several of the games can be expanded or combined with another one. This will allow several variations and new possibilities.

The diagram below gives a quick overview and shows the combinations of the different games.

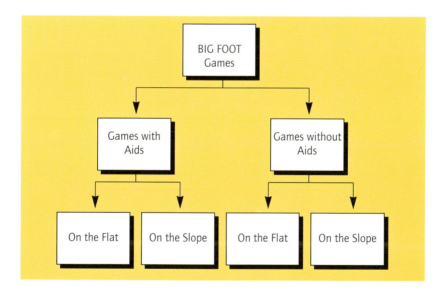

We have divided BIG FOOT games into two categories:

1) Games without aids (including ski sticks).
2) Games with aids.

In both categories we differentiate between games on the flat and games on the slope. There are several games shown as examples for each category. The different character of each game is important and this determines its use and selected category. There are games to be played with or against each other, and there are games which can be played individually. In this way the games encourage creativity, possess a competitive spirit, and above all are confidence building. Some games require a quiet spot or at least an area not often used for skiing. Early on keep an eye out for such suitable spots and do not forget the weather gods in your planning. They have often ruined even the best ideas with fog, snow drifts or simply just damnably cold spells.

Games on Flat Snow without Aids

Relay Races on the Flat

Divide yourselves up into teams and line up alongside each other. The aim of the game, played on flat ground, is to get round a marker or a hazard by using any form of forward movement. Each member of the team does the circuit and sends off the next man by touching him to go. Relay races can be expanded by adding any kind of variation onto the basic game.

One variation, for example, is the wheelbarrow. One person from each team supports himself on a set of BIG FOOT using his hands and is pushed along by the legs by another player.

Target group: Very good for children, but also for grown-ups who are beginners.
When to use: Specifically for beginners on the first day, or subsequently at the beginning of each session, or as a warming-up exercise.

BIGFOOT

Catching and Throwing Games

Catching and throwing can be easily arranged and could include games such as 'tag', 'pass the parcel', 'catch' etc. Everyone knows these games and even grown-ups like to be reminded of their childhood. Things can be made straight forward by marking out a play area or court using rucksacks, articles of clothing and this does nottake up much time. For 'catch' you can use a snowball. However the players heads are taboo as a target – most people do not enjoy receiving a hard snowball directly in the face! You can also play these games in teams. A snowball fight on BIG FOOT is also fun and practises your balance, braking and gliding without your realising it.

> **Target group:** Depending on the type of game, usable for any group, but especially suitable for children.
> **When to use:** Use as a warming-up exercise and for beginner's training.

Dancing on the BIG FOOT

Dancing is a fun way of doing warming-up exercises which also brings out the thespian traits in one. Dancing has no boundaries – you can go from normal dancing to group choreography. For a musical accompaniment you can either sing or improvise using simple 'instruments' such as the comb, bells or ski sticks.

If you are lucky to find a suitable location, for example in front of a ski hut, you may be able to use their music at no cost.

> **Target group:** There is no particular group in mind but suitable for ski course groups.
> **When to use:** Use as a warming-up exercise or 'cooling off' exercise at the end of a session.

BIGFOOT

BIG FOOT

Gymnastics and Stretching Exercises with BIG FOOT

One can carry out gymnastics in a fun way starting with a song or a story and then moving on to warm-up the most important sets of muscles. This is much more fun than the traditional methods. Specific exercises for stretching can be built into these fun sessions. The usual way of warming-up, often laughed at, can nevertheless prove to be more motivating and can even be carried out wearing your BIG FOOT. One example could be – imagine Paul Schockemöhle or Michael Whittacker on their horses, or use the scenario of a Hickstead Horse Show.

The group is standing round in a circle and one of them tells a story which then has to be played out by the group. This is a simple idea and can be varied as one wishes. Everyone takes part in the 'horse show' and tries to 'jump' a clear round. You 'trot' into the arena and halt in front of the judges where you make a big bow. The time starts now. A quick gallop to the first jump and then onto the parallel bars, which must be cleared, and then again onto the treble bar combination after a short left turn, then comes the water jump, and so on and so forth ...

A favourite variation is to use pop songs with lots of rhythm such as the song "We will rock you" by the Queen pop group. You all stand in a circle and clap hands alternately slapping your thighs with two strokes and then the hands. Another idea is to sing variations of well-known songs adapted to reflect the BIG FOOT theme e.g., The Happy Wanderer:

> "I love to go a BIG FOOTing,
> along the mountain track,
> and as I go I love to sing
> My BIG FOOT on my back
> Tra la la Tra la li
> Tra la la Tra la la la la la la la etc., ...
> My BIG FOOT on my back

Doing your stretching exercises with your BIG FOOT strapped on is, as we have said earlier, perfectly feasible. This presents no problem whether you are doing straight forward exercises of your calf or thigh muscles, or whether you need to exercise other more complicated parts of the body. You will know these from other types of sport. Note, however, that according to the type of piste you are skiing on the leg muscles are the important ones. You should concentrate on this point. The main thing is that you should warm-up first and then not overdo your stretching exercises. Otherwise, if it is really icy cold, there is a grave danger of causing injury when doing the stretching exercises. An alternative, therefore, is to ski slowly and warm-up that way.

Stretching Exercises - but which Ones?

1) Stretching the inside of the legs.
2) Stretching your calf muscles.
3) To do stretching exercises of the thigh muscles a partner comes in very handy - see the photographs on the next page.

Target group: Suitable for everybody.
When to use: When warming-up.

Games in the Snow without Aids on the Slope

Relay Races on the Slope

Organising relay races on the side of a slope is the same as doing them on the flat. The race can be run down the slope or across the slope. The terrain in this case offers a possibility to alternate between uphill and downhill skiing as well as being able to use the gradient of the slope itself. Well-known children's games e.g., 'grandma's footsteps', are very useful

BIGFOOT

and above all give you the training in basic principles – in this case – braking. The participants all stand next to each other on the slope. One person stands about 20 metres in front of the rest and looks down into the valley with his back to the group. He counts up to five, out loud, before turning round. While he is counting, the group skis down to try to touch the 'counter'. When he turns round everyone must stop immediately. If anyone moves they must climb back up to be the last person. The 'counter' slides 3 metres further down the slope each time after he has turned round. The first one to reach the counter before he turns round takes over the role of the counter.

Target group: Children and beginners.
When to use: When warming-up and during basic training of techniques.

BIG FOOT

Stretching the inside of the legs.

Stretching your calf muscles.

To do stretching exercises of the thigh muscles a partner comes in very handy.

Tasks and Playing

There are many possibilities.

First of all we speak of tasks which are complementary to the main exercise but which have a playful character. Here are a few examples:

- Ski down the slope gathering up as much snow as you can in order to make a snowball. Now throw the snowball upwards, or at a target.
- Ski down the slope and throw a snowball at a partner so that he can catch it without it breaking up.
- Ski as a group down the slope as if you were tracing out the shape of a star.

Target group: Children and advanced beginners.
When to use: During the training of techniques.

Secondly, there are tasks which, with imagination and fantasy, introduce new forms of movement. Examples are:

BIG FOOT

- Ski like a robot ... or like a dwarf ... or like - whatever you like.
- Imagine you are a giant when you have completed your swing turn ... or like a dwarf when you are steering into a turn, or ... and so on ...
- Ski arrogantly, ski as if you were drunk or tired or and so on ... !
- ... or like a musician?

Target group: Grown-ups.
When to use: During the training of techniques, or when warming-up.

Playing with the Swing

Games doing the swing are done mainly when skiing downhill. These games can be used to expand on new ideas or replace the simpler games we have mentioned earlier. One of the most interesting games using the swing, and which is at the same time extremely good training, is the human slalom. This is considerably easier to do on BIG FOOT than on alpine skis. One's reaction is sharper on BIG FOOT and collisions can easily be avoided. To do the human slalom the whole group lines up down the slope, each sliding down so that there is a distance of 5-7 metres difference between each of them. The one highest up goes through the slalom and ends up at the same distance as the others but now at the bottom end of the group. Each person can go through several times. This way you can ski all the way down a long slope. The advantage over free skiing is that the turns you have to do are predetermined. The distance between the 'human' gates can be varied just as one wishes.

Target group: All BIG FOOT groups.
When to use: During the training of techniques, and to increase motivation.

BIG FOOT

Games with the Swing

The fun character of BIG FOOT skiing now reaches its high point. First of all we want to give some examples of games with the swing which serve, on the one hand, to give clarity to the principles of the swing and assist in training, and on the other hand encourage you to try out your own swing movements according to your own imagination.

The Aeroplane

Use your outstretched arms to represent the wings. By dipping the one 'wing' you automatically turn into the swing. Executing a long curve turn is particular fun with this game.

Target group:	Children and grown-ups, advanced beginners.
When to use:	During the training of techniques, or when warming-up.

The Marmot

Everyone turns into a little marmot and acts out this story:

We are all little marmots and first of all crouch low down in our den as we traverse across the slope. In order that we can keep watch for our enemy we slowly stretch ourselves up in the air as we turn downhill, putting up our hands to pretend they are our ears, and then freeze holding our body stiff. When we see the hunter we shrink down low quickly and turn our legs in the new direction.

Target group:	Children, grown-ups, beginners and advanced skiers.
When to use:	During the training of techniques, when warming-up or to loosen up.

The Boxer

Begin the swing turn on easy terrain, skiing downhill. By slightly raising up the 'cover' arm, and following this by throwing a punch diagonally with the other, you will automatically execute a curve swing. Change over your 'boxing' cover and the punching arm alternately.

Target group:	Children, grown-ups and advanced beginners.
When to use:	During the training of the swing technique for shortish turns.

The Running Swing

The running swing is one of nicest swing games on the BIG FOOT. This game makes the advantages of BIG FOOT particularly clear. By slowly dragging one foot forward then the other (similar to the skating gait downhill), and combined with a swinging of the arms across the body, one again automatically moves into a turn as one unweights the feet.

BIGFOOT

Target group: Children, grown-ups and advanced beginners.
When to use: During the training of techniques, or when warming-up.

Dancing with BIG FOOT

Dancing on the slope with BIG FOOT is similar in character to ice dancing. One dances down the slope – on one's own, in pairs or as a group. Your fantasy will know no boundaries. It is probably the greatest bit of fun that you will experience on BIG FOOT.

Various specialities can be combined with dancing such as pirouettes, moving backwards, gliding on one leg, or the 'inside-BIG FOOT-swing', where you ski on the outside edge of the uphill-BIG FOOT.

Other variations include e.g., deliberately falling down and then picking yourself up and carrying on, or you can use gymnastic movements such as the forward roll in the snow.

BIG FOOT

The most well-known dance is the waltz. Humming the three-quarter rhythm melody – off we go. Two or more skiers hold hands and turning in a circle, dance down the slope. You can dance arms apart or close together – just as you wish.

> **Target group:** Children, grown-ups, beginners and advanced beginners.
> **When to use:** As a speciality for loosening up and for balance training.

Lots and Lots of BIG FOOT: Building Formations

Skiing in Formation

Skiing in formation demands synchronisation of all the participants' movements. This is quite easy on BIG FOOT, and one can ski very close together doing it. Irrespective of whether the group members ski one behind the other, next to each other, stay in the same track or trace figures in the snow, skiing in formation is fun and provides good reaction training. One can incorporate dance or gymnastic movements into the fun and this makes it similar to 'freestyle' dancing.

Some examples which are also suitable for beginners are as follows:
- The caterpillar: Done on skis this counts as a 'knee jerker', but on BIG FOOT it is real fun.
- Synchronised skiing in pairs.
- As a threesome it is a lot more difficult!

BIGFOOT

Whether you ski next to each other, or behind one another there is a multitude of variations. The more complex formations are more suitable for competent skiers. Skiing across each other, like the motor cycle display team, starts with three of you trying it out and moving on to an endless number of people.

Take Care! This last formation carries with it a high risk of a crash.

Target group:	Suitable for all.
When to use:	Use as a speciality or for balance and rhythm training.

Games on Flat Snow with Aids

Warming-up exercises as a group can be turned into fun by using a few accoutrements from other games. These must, however, be small in size and easily transportable in a rucksack. Balloons, tennis or rubber balls, any other small balls, straps, rope and also frisbees are most suitable in this respect.

All the known catching, throwing as well as team games can be carried out on BIG FOOT either with or without a competitive spirit. You could try tug-of-war which will give you a new feeling of gliding and provides training for your edging exercises. Also there is the game where you try to collect as many straps as you can which are hanging out of peoples' pockets.

Another game is to try to knock a big light ball over a line by throwing snowballs at it – however, the score will not be as great as in soccer. Nevertheless, using simple equipment and aids, one can create a lot of fun and in turn, by using such accessories, you will have unwittingly introduced movement training into the session.

Target group:	Children, grown-ups, beginners and the advanced.
When to use:	For warming up and to motivate.

Games in the Snow with Aids on the Slope

The most important aid, when playing various games, are your ski sticks and also bits of your clothing which are not important, such as a ski hat or a scarf. Taking poles with you is a little bit cumbersome. However these can be used universally and can be fun. You can add to your list of aids as you wish. Sometimes ideas devised on the spur of the moment, or borne out of necessity are just as good as planned methods, and will take care of all eventualities.

Picking up Objects

Picking up objects constitute simple games on the slope. One of you skis off and as he is moving he drops something (e.g., a pair of gloves, ski hat etc.,). Either one of you, or several of you, then ski after him collecting up the 'lost' items. Speed, as well as the distance between the 'lost' items, can be varied according to the ability of the group members.

Target Group:	Children, grown-ups, beginners and the advanced.
When to use:	To exercise techniques and reaction training.

Jumping Games

Lay out a number of objects down the slope. Each of you must now try to jump over them as you ski down. The objects can be laid out to create and train a particular rhythm – or they can be laid out just haphazardly in order to exercise reaction and timing. The games can be expanded to include little relay races or synchronised jumping.

BIGFOOT

BIG FOOT

Target group:	Children, grown-ups, beginners as well as the advanced.
When to use:	As a diversion, or to train reaction or techniques.

Games with the Swing, Dancing and Running Blindfold

At this juncture we will borrow from someone else. Walter Kuchler describes a number of games using the swing in his book 'Skizirkus'. His ideas can be used to much more effect on BIG FOOT than on alpine skis. Here are a few examples:

The Head Waiter Swing

To do the head waiter swing you hold your ski sticks in front of you, at chest height, as if they were a tray of drinks. The 'waiter' skis off in medium sized swinging movements down the slope. He 'serves' the drinks out always with his tray on the downhill side. Each time he has served a drink and then executes a turn his 'tray' must be on the right hand side and then be changed over to be on the left hand side.

The Dwarf Swing

Grip the ski sticks half way down the poles. Automatically your body will be crouched smaller. When doing short swings you will stay in this posture. Adjustable telescopic ski sticks available for BIG FOOT are most suitable for this exercise as they allow you to hold the ski sticks more firmly.

The Stretcher Bearer Swing

You can ski down in pairs, one behind the other, carrying a 'stretcher' using ski sticks or a couple of poles to represent the stretcher. One particular 'kick' can be achieved if one of the bearers is blindfolded.

BIGFOOT

The Head Waiter Swing

The Dwarf Swing

The Stretcher Bearer Swing

Waltzing in pairs with ski sticks

Waltzing in pairs with ski sticks

Waltzing with ski sticks is a well-liked method on ski courses. Each dancer grips the opposite ends of the ski sticks and they turn each other as they ski down the slope. Be careful to make sure that the sticks are gripped firmly – it is safer to do it with poles.

Target group:	Children, grown-ups, beginners as well as the advanced.
When to use:	To train reaction or for motivation.

BIGFOOT

Slalom and Obstacle Courses

Instead of marking the slalom gates by using people you can mark the course out by using objects or poles. Using these aids allows one to drive at the gates with more aggression. A highpoint for experts is to use the flexible marker poles which you can brush aside with the outside hand as you negotiate them (see chapter 9 'With BIG FOOT amongst the Slalom Poles').

On top of this you can erect obstacles using for example ski sticks which you have to either negotiate or jump over.

Target group: Children, grown-ups, beginners and the advanced.

When to use: To train reaction and techniques, and generally for fun.

- BIG FOOT Rallying

 Day on BIG FOOT – just for Fun!

A BIG FOOT rally can consist of any of the games we have mentioned as well as include those you have made up yourself. Several groups, moving off together, have to solve particular tasks one after the other. If you wear fancy dress the fun is more than doubled. The big advantage of doing a skiing rally on BIG FOOT is that you do not have the problem of having to remove your skis because your newly achieved manoeuvrability makes this unnecessary. You can easily carry out the exciting tasks which have been set. These do not necessarily always have to be centred around skiing on BIG FOOT. Orders for the day such as "Do everything backwards!", can set the fantasy racing and can lead to often unbelievable challenges.

BIG FOOT

In order to give you some idea how a BIG FOOT rally would look like here are some organisational tips.

It is a certainty that you will spontaneously come up with some ideas of your own during the planning.

A BIG FOOT rally should take into account a group size of at least 20 people in order to ensure that the effort placed in organising it is in relation to the fun accomplished. Do not underestimate the effort you will have to put in to organising one. The work can be simplified by setting up an organising committee. This should be done at the beginning of the winter holiday so that there is enough time allowed for the planning to be carried out. Also think of refreshments for the group out on the slope, as this must be bought beforehand.

The timing of the event is best arranged to coincide with local festivities e.g., the 'Bergfest' – which takes place also about half way through your holiday. Alternatively a good time is the last day on BIG FOOT on the holiday.

As a general principle the organising committee should ensure that the aim of making the rally fun for all members of the group is maintained, and that everyone is included in the event. This automatically makes the selection of tasks concerning skill account for all the varying standards of the participants e.g., so that children and beginners alike can do them.

The piste course chosen should be a simple slope giving vantage points where all the task points can be seen by all the group members who will want to watch others as they go round. A variation on the theme is an 'orienteering' event in the local ski area. Similarly the route chosen should be suitable and the terrain easily passable by all members of the group.

An additional element of fun can be achieved by using a mixture of BIG FOOT skiing and quizzes. An example of such a mixture looks like this

BIG FOOT

1. Select the members for each group at random.

2. Spread out the tasks giving timings and routes.

3. Get each group to choose a motto for themselves according to their dress e.g., sheikhs, dustmen with rubbish bags etc.

4. Get the groups to tell everyone what their 'war-cry' is.

5. The ski route to the event.

6. Description of the task at each of the event points e.g., ski down the slope with a plastic beaker full of water. Which group arrives at the finish with the most water? ... All kinds of relay races ... and so on ...

7. Lunch on the piste (or in the ski hut) with a general quiz competition or tasks such as Trivial Pursuit, cards and so on ...

8. Games for the group on the piste: Which group can lay out the longest line of clothing without taking-off the main ski outfit? The whole group has to cover a stretch of 20 metres using only four BIG FOOT between them ...

9. A spot for the artists. Which group can make the best-looking or the biggest snowman? Allow time for the qroups to practise the acting of a song or a funny story to be given at the evening party.

10. Act out the song or funny story in front of a judging panel.

11. Prize-giving and party.

Showing a video recording of the highlights of the BIG FOOT rally prior to the prize-giving can serve to put everyone in the party mood.

7 'IT DOES NOT ALWAYS HAVE TO BE TWO METRES LONG' – POSSIBILITIES FOR THE BIG FOOT CONNOISSEUR

"BIG FOOT ? Ah, well, it is all very well to show-off - I would rather go skiing." In the past, we heard this kind of remark quite often whenever we were trying to persuade someone to take up BIG FOOT. We will now tell you what the connoisseur will miss, however, if he does not at least have a go. This does not mean that we want to put you under pressure to make a choice between BIG FOOT or alpine skis. Rather more we want to show you the possibilities that exist where the characteristics of BIG FOOT can be used to improve your ski techniques. If you do not try them, you will be missing out – most certainly with all the fun.

'Steep Slope, Moguls, Halfpipes? – And?'

Whether you are pressing on down a mogul stretch, successfully mastering a steep slope without fear, or mixing together with others in 'snowboarder paradise', simply getting to know your 'one-board' colleagues, then with BIG FOOT there will be a whole lot of new experiences open to you.

Differing types of terrain require you to employ different techniques. These are also in the main applicable and common to skiing, where they can be used equally as well. The big advantage with BIG FOOT is that you can get to know new types of movement without, in the worse case, having any painful experiences. Later this gives you the confidence to try out skiing movements.

There you are in the middle of it all, and almost as if you are were standing in a door-frame, you feel as if you could steady yourself with your hand against the slope. It could be that it is all rather narrow – perhaps as little as 3 metres wide – and you will need to execute a turn – this is a big challenge, even for the expert. You will not have to wait long before you will have to go through this kind of thrilling experience.

BIGFOOT

Steep Slope

With shivers running down your spine as you look down – and it is nothing to do with the weather.

On the steep slope it is not skiing along that is the dangerous thing – more the risk of crashing out, coupled with the danger of sliding afterwards. As you strive, with all your energy to stop, you notice, with an uneasy feeling, that the speed was too great and this was downright dangerous. Perhaps you should give up trying to get an entry in the Guinness Book of Records for the longest slide in ski clothing!

If you get involved in such a slide it is the objects which lie in your path that are the danger (people, stones, rocks) as they lie in wait for you. Therefore the motto is to go slowly and risk nothing. However if it does happen that you unwittingly get into such an embarrassing position, and you find yourself slipping and sliding down the slope, turn yourself round as quickly as possible so that your BIG FOOT are downhill, and jam your inside and outside edges deep into the slope so that you are able to effect a halt.

Above all you should work out what caused your crash. There are various mistakes that you will not want to repeat. The most common fault is leaning too far into the hillside. You tend to do this rather instinctively. It is really quite important, especially on a very steep slope, to lean downhill, keep a forward stance, and as you go along keep looking downhill so that you can keep your BIG FOOT upright and running true. Using the whole width of the piste, and making small radius turns, will help you to maintain a controllable speed the first time you try a slope. You will note that once you have conquered your first BIG FOOT steep slope everything else will be considerably simpler.

Moguls

"Always keep contact with the snow! Keep your legs relaxed! Control speed! Bend your body forward etc.!" Always a plethora of tips. A never-ending list of factors to take into consideration. And all on 2 m long skis? Anyone who has already tried a mogul slope knows this kind of situation. Full of good resoluteness – and after a couple of turns …! Nevertheless mastery of the moguls remains the ace of techniques for skiers, and is a challenge of one's fitness and condition. All the moguls met must be compensated for and this is done by the legs.

Why then do we bother to ski with BIG FOOT on mogul terrain? Because by doing so we can easily improve our speed of reaction a lot and give us experience. One of the problems encountered on skis – easily twisting the leg – is totally avoided on BIG FOOT. So let's keep our BIG FOOT pointing downhill and watch out for what is coming up next. It is still quite possible to ski a turn or two in mogul terrain.

A skier would not be able to match this. New dimensions are opened up as you come to terms with this form of terrain and these will pay off later as you return to using skis. Just like other characteristics, crashing out in mogul terrain is half as bad on BIG FOOT. The odd stunt or so can usually be carried off without injury.

The tactics and techniques, using BIG FOOT, hardly differ from the normal way of tackling mogul country. With soft moguls you will have to be careful that you do not stick your 'big toe' in.

Basically there are three ways of attacking moguls:
1. You go downhill around each mogul.
2. You ski the slant sides of the mogul, cutting the sides.
3. You ski over the top of the mogul.

Combining all the possibilities 'dive through the archway' and ski down a set of moguls. To change direction use various different swing methods. It is well worth trying a mixture of the individual swing types (see chapter 8 'Classic' Swing Techniques). For practice, so that you can keep up with skiers later on, here's a tip: before getting onto the slope work out a route down which is as near as possible to the fall line.

Just imagine you are running down a narrow one yard wide lane, and you see a barrel that is filling up the width of the lane coming towards you. In order to clear the barrel you pull your legs up just before it reaches you and jump over it, stretching your legs down again for the landing. This is how you can tackle the individual moguls you meet. Except that you should really be trying to keep your feet in contact with the snow – which means not jumping.

When you are on the top of the mogul your upper body should be at the same height as it normally is when you are on the flat. In extreme cases only your knees will be up somewhere round your ears. The legs function in this case like shock absorbers. In order to regain balance and get your compressed legs straight again, press down your legs in the flat area after the mogul. Just imagine you are trying to stub out a cigarette with your heel. The stretching motion should be done alternately, left and then right, so that you can carry out various swinging movements.

You can also even conquer high moguls on BIG FOOT.

In order to get a feeling of rhythm and be able to strengthen your ski parallel you can try out a few slopes using ski sticks. In this way you will be forced to use an upright posture. The feeling you get doing this will be similar to normal skiing, and will give you some exercise in the use of ski sticks. In the upright position the ski sticks will give the necessary support.

Halfpipes and other Snowboarding Territory

Using BIG FOOT in the halfpipe – the long semi-elliptical snow gully with its two walls each side – you can ski up and along its banking almost vertically. Nowadays there are specially constructed parks which have been prepared by snowplough expressly for this purpose and to satisfy snowboarders. There is only one rule for doing the halfpipe: try out BIG FOOT on anything that looks like fun.

Skiing up the banking in the halfpipe calls, initially, for a little bit of courage, until you can gradually reach the upper limits of the sides.

If you have misjudged your approach speed into the Halfpipe, on BIG FOOT you always will be able to react quickly.

BIGFOOT

Whoops! First attempt at the Halfpipe. It looks very scary, but as a rule it all comes off OK in the end and without injury. Usually crashes are not dangerous and all that will happen is that you slip down the slope of the tunnel. On skis, situations like these can lead to an involuntary exit out over the top of the Halfpipe lip. An experiment of this kind is therefore not recommended.

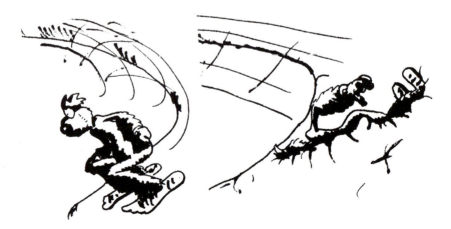

It is all very similar to the toboggan run. In some skiing resorts it is quite common to find snow packed up to create a run, where the curves, formed by the gradient of the walls, have to be negotiated by using a lot of inner edge. You can practise your 'aeroplane' swing learned earlier on.

When you sniff around the snowboard haunts it will occur to you that on BIG FOOT you attack the various types of ground more in the manner of a skier. The relativity of spectacular acrobatics to freestyle stunts is similar, as in the past, between skate-boarders and roller-skaters using the wooden 'Halfpipe' ramps.

If it could be said that skate-boarders are potential snowboarders, then it will be true that, with the appearance on the scene of the BIG FOOT model 'TRICK', many in-line skaters will be, in the future, conquering the slopes on BIG FOOT. Because it is very suitable for doing the Halfpipe, 'BIG FOOT TRICK' users can already do some spectacular manoeuvres. If you get a move on perhaps you will belong to the new generation for this event.

BIGFOOT

8 BIG FOOT AND "CLASSIC" SWING TECHNIQUES – INCOMPATIBLE?

What has BIG FOOT to do with 'classical' ski techniques? This is a simple question answered rapidly. For anyone who wants to use BIG FOOT, not only just for fun, it offers itself as an aid to improve your skiing ability further. In areas where skiers find little difficulties, blind spots or even inhibitions holding them back from trying out things, or collecting experiences on unknown terrain, BIG FOOT can very often give them an easier way of getting on.

Let's look at an example. You have been trying to learn to do the short swing turn on the last few winter holidays. What looks so simple, as other skiers do it on the piste, should after all be learnable by yourself ... but. ...
Whatever you do, and however hard you try, it simply will not function. This is where BIG FOOT comes in. Strap them on and you will soon find out that with their particular characteristics the short swing turn will very quickly be a possibility.

This however, does not mean that the same turn will immediately be possible on the 'long planks'. But something positive and important has already happened. You have a better feeling for what the swing turn is like, because you have been able to experience it – first hand.

In this manner you can gather all the valuable experience of the movements, which will be extremely necessary to further your learning. Of course, BIG FOOT is no panacea – but it surely is a valuable complementary aid for reaching new dimensions of experience. In such cases, by the way, it is advisable to use ski sticks so that their functionality is also included in the various techniques.

In the following pages we are going to give some short descriptions of the most important of the 'classical' and 'modern' BIG FOOT swing techniques and illustrate their uses.

The Rotation Technique

The most important feature of all the swings, using the rotation technique, is the turning of the body in a new direction. When the turn of the upper body is blocked by the hips the turning impulse is transmitted to the skis. This is equally so whether you are moving on BIG FOOT or normal skis. Just try it out.

Traversing across the slope, pull the uphill shoulder back ready for the swing turn. Now turn the upper body in the new direction. In this way the movement runs from the shoulder to the hips and over the knees to the BIG FOOT. By blocking this movement at the hips the swing will be directly transmitted onto the ski equipment.

You stoop down deep into the swing turn and enjoy the exhilarating feeling of your posture in the turn. BIG FOOT in particular gives you a good sense of the way the hip block works. The body movement is carried out momentarily and the change of direction follows promptly.

The rotation technique has a special meaning particularly in deep snow. However, since these sort of conditions are not good for BIG FOOT we'll leave this kind of swing technique to the skiers.

Leg Extension Technique

Although in recent years medical opinion has brought this method into disrepute, the leg extension technique is the way to carry out the short swing turn. It allows one to carry out a repetitive rhythmic swinging movement. To learn this method on normal skis takes a lot of time, however the incentive to learn it is greater and skiers put medical opinion to the back of their minds and disregard it. The basic movement of this kind is the 'up extension'. To start the swing turn as one traverses, both legs push up from the ground simultaneously. As the body stretches up the skis begin to turn. Your bottom turns during the swing in the opposite direction to the legs. The 'cranking' movement of the knees is more pronounced as one stoops down in the steering phase that follows. To counter balance the legs, which are turned in uphill in the turn, the upper body leans forwards and downhill. In order to be able to maintain your direction the downhill ski takes all the weight and the edging grip is dug in deeper.

Certainly the most attractive of the up extension swing turns is created by skiing down in a zigzag manner. By using a series of rapidly executed up extensions, one after the other, and by keeping your skis flat, you ski downhill like a gliding serpent. If you swing from edge to edge dynamically you will be able to do the short swing turn.

BIG FOOT is useful in learning or to improve the leg extension techniques since there is reduced resistance on the skis. To be able to get into the rhythm of the short swing, as far as we are concerned, you can use any aid. BIG FOOT allows a safe controllable speed to be employed. The requirement to unweight the skis a lot - unavoidable when using alpine skis - is reduced to a minimum. Because of this you can concentrate on the actual sequence of the movements so that you can make them more effective.

BIGFOOT

BIGFOOT

All short swing turns can be carried out with or without ski sticks.

Equally the steadying swing belongs to the leg extension group. This particular swing, which is very necessary when negotiating moguls, can be easily optimised using BIG FOOT.

Side-slipping Technique

This swing technique stems from ski racing. The development of the flexible slalom marking pole means that it is no longer necessary to have to ski with the body right round the pole. Since it is more convenient, now that you only have to bring the skis round the pole, while the body goes over it or 'through' the pole, it is similar to a swing which stems from general movements that you make every day. While traversing, the downhill ski is pushed forward and the downhill arm falls rearwards, at the same time the uphill arm is brought forward and the change of balance is made off the leg which is still the uphill one. In other words, so far, it is no different than the movements in a normal walking gait, with the cross over co-ordination of arms and legs. By dipping the body into the swing turn more pressure is brought onto the edges of the skis. The equipment's natural running line forces you into the swing. The correction comes by placing the inside foot alongside the other. During the whole movement there is no wrenching of the knee joint.

The side-slipping technique is a gentle one despite its close relationship to ski racing. A further advantage is that the energy required to carry it out is well within limits, since one can ski without a great deal of unweighting of the equipment. The whole swing movement relies on the natural steering qualities of the ski itself. This is more than very similar, of course, with our BIG FOOT. Running on the edges is a particular speciality. Just rely totally on your BIG FOOT's ability, and using this technique you will arrive at the bottom of the piste quickly, safely and without having to expend a lot of energy.

The technical challenges facing skiers these days have been lessened because of the development in skiing equipment – the skis are constantly being made narrower. Material takes on an ever increasingly important role. The so-called radial technique has been developed based on this factor. The swing turn in this case is carried out on the edges of the ski right from the start of the turn. This system of 'riding on the edges' (carving) is also the main feature of the BIG FOOT swing (see chapter 11 'The Swing à la BIG FOOT').

Of course the swing techniques described only represent a selection. There are a multitude of other steering and change of direction methods. It has been our aim, at this juncture, to give you advice on some examples where BIG FOOT can be a benefit and offer assistance so that you can experience relatively difficult movements.

9 WITH BIG FOOT AMONGST THE SLALOM POLES

 seconds!

Your time is always an objective target and an exciting element by which to measure your performance with others. There is nothing wrong in this. It is a good feeling to be able to be quicker, or to work up and get close to a target best time, and this is just as valid whether you are using alpine skis or BIG FOOT. Besides the fun and excitement of being able to ski down a slalom course faster than others, there is another function at question. You can certainly improve your manoeuvrability by skiing a slalom or obstacle course – a target which again shows up the advantages of your BIG FOOT.

Even at international level it is no secret that national teams from a number of different countries can be seen strapping on BIG FOOT. They use them during special training sessions to improve their skiing line and leg strength, and to quicken up their reaction timing.

What is good enough for top skiers should be good for us also. However, what advantages are there for us by doing slalom training with BIG FOOT, besides those mentioned above? The new point is that we are now being forced to ski in a particular track. What effect this has on your skiing style can be soon experienced when you emerge out of the forest of slalom poles and find yourself on open ground again. Apart from this it is simply a lot of fun to concentrate on doing the slalom for a whole day. Comparing your times on the runs you are able to improve your feeling for the movements, your various tactics, your attack line and use of the ground. The other advantage of BIG FOOT is that, despite all the threading in and out of the poles, you will seldom crash out (BIG FOOT-ers use the term 'slam'). You are able to make good use of the opportunity to train your reaction if the poles are placed very – even extremely – close together. You will experience a real buzz and, despite the excitement, will be able to have the chance to conquer the 'forest' of poles.

BIGFOOT

Equipment

The simplest form of slalom, using a minimum of equipment, is the human slalom. Members of the group take turns in acting as the poles. A slalom using ski sticks is also one way of creating a course with little trouble. However, using the proper slalom poles makes the whole thing more exciting and realistic. For the expert the whole thing only begins when the correct professional equipment is in place. To get the most fun out of this 'forest of poles', the use of flexible poles is an absolute must.

After the first 'touch', as you round the poles, you begin to realise how much courage and concentration it takes to really 'attack' them so aggressively to make up that hundredth of a second.

Irrespective of whether you use the knee-high poles or the full length ones, the challenge remains the same. If you have protective pads available to wear, you will be able to really 'go' at the poles.

All this kind of equipment – and here is the real problem – is not usually available for hire. Improvisation is therefore the watchword. You should wear unbreakable ski goggles to avoid the odd black eye, at least for the first few attempts. Instead of using protectors, or padded ski gloves, you can knock the poles away as you round them using the ski stick. If you do not use ski sticks, like slalom snowboarders for example, then you definitely need to wear elbow protectors. A small piece of flat wood taped to the lower side of the arm can serve this purpose. Also soccer players' shin-pads, strapped again to the underarm, make contact with the poles less painful. You can look really professional if you wear the proper shin-pads. A missed pole can be swept aside simply

BIG FOOT

with the knees. You can get by using a second pair of soccer players' shin-pads as knee protection. The motto is 'well-padded' up makes it easier to 'dance' through the forest of poles.

Course Building

The first questions you will be asking yourself are – where am I allowed to mark out a slalom course? – Which piste is suitable for it? The basic principle is to ask either the lift personnel or contact the local ski school, preferably a day beforehand. Both of these sources will be able to tell you whether you may mark out a course at all, which part of the piste you may use, and certainly which piste is best suitable. Experience shows that the most suitable courses are erected on short runs, alongside which there is a short tow or chairlift. This gives you the opportunity to watch what others are doing and to be able do quick turn rounds. As regards the distance between slalom poles, for BIG FOOT slaloms there is no norm. Indeed, when you try for the first time to mark out a nice straightforward slalom you will learn that it is quite an art.

A few tips for you to take note of:

Every 5-8 metres place a pole in a corridor up to 3 metres wide. It is up to you and your imagination to make variations for longer or shorter corners, or to make a course for symmetric or asymmetric rhythms. Depending on your intention you can construct your BIG FOOT course to concentrate on testing skill, running ability or specific events such as a medium slalom, a giant slalom, or a specially constructed BIG FOOT course with narrow gates.

Slalom Skills

The slalom, aimed to test your skilfulness, can be done by anyone – one can always work at improving one's skill. Doing this kind of slalom your skill can be improved either by the way the gates and boundaries are set, or by the difficulty of skill required at each of the gates. For the expert skiers here are a few ways to give yourself new challenges in differing skills for the slalom:

1. Differently angled gates
2. Predetermined skiing lines
3. Preset handicaps

In case 1 above, place the gate poles in the snow at differing diagonal angles. You will automatically train yourself in the different skiing techniques when you are running between gates, where the tips of the poles are angled in towards you like a roof, or where the poles are set so obliquely that you have to take a wide swing out to avoid touching the tips of the poles.

Predetermined skiing lines means that, besides the radius of the turns, a line has been laid down which you must keep to. Additional boundaries can be laid down which you are also not allowed to ski over. This often demands a more accurate skiing line to be taken. You will either be forced to execute swing turns at a particular point or get to a predetermined distance away from the poles.

One extreme pre-determined skiing line is, for example, the '360 degree' turn round a pole thus forcing a loop.

The third possibility to make the slalom more interesting is to make up a small selection of handicaps. This could be going backwards, going on one leg, using a swing turn on the inside leg and so on and so forth ... It is quite fun to think up even more difficult situations which you can use to go through the gates. Perhaps one of the biggest challenges is to go on one leg through narrowly placed gates made of knee-height poles.

Equally a high standard of skill is demanded skiing through gates which have been joined together, with plastic tapeon, the downhill line. This means that after each turn you have to include a jump as well.

Slalom in Difficult Terrain

Marking out and doing a slalom on for example, difficult terrain such as a mogul stretch on normal skis is reserved at best for a few of the top skiers. Doing the same on BIG FOOT, of course, makes it much, much more difficult, but it is a possibility.

Mogul terrain forms the extreme of the variations with which you will come to terms with and can be seen, at the same time, as a test of your progress. There are, however, other more simpler forms of terrain such as undulating ground, overhangs, banking and runs down over escarpments where you can mark out your first slalom on difficult terrain.

Once you have decided on a special piece of ground, you will soon notice that you will have to put a great deal of thought into the different ways of marking it out. He who calls the tune pays the piper!

Here are a few suggestions on where to place the gates:
- on the top of a mogul
- on the flank side of a mogul
- immediately after a mogul
- on the tip of, or in the dead ground after undulating ground etc.

Different forms of terrain, or predetermined tracks, demand different techniques. On slaloms with different types and variations of gates you will notice automatically which technique could improve your time. Slaloms, where there are little slides and jumps, including ones which involve jump turns, add an additional thrill. Your jumping prowess and techniques will soon match the challenges you face.

If you are looking to make direct visible comparisons on who is fastest or who has the steadier nerves, then the **parallel slalom** (i.e., in twos) is the only way. It has been made very popular by snowboarders in recent years and is certainly more fun than trying to beat your own time all the time. You can use this type of slalom to good effect for a ski rally.

Having described the equipment and the marking out of your course, now some words on tactics and techniques for the slalom.

Tactics and Techniques

First of all the slalom must, of course, match the level of competence of the skier. You have already learned the variations possible. So we know already that different types of terrain demand different techniques. Techniques to match terrain were included earlier in detail in individual sections (e.g., 'BIG FOOT and Moguls').

Now we want to give you some tips for skiing on a slippery slope. In principle, when marking out the gates, you should vary them, using a mixture of glide sections, steep parts as well as giant slalom. This will require each skier to use a varying tactical approach.

We have noticed on various slalom courses that the swing for the next gate is invariably made too late. On BIG FOOT, at speed down the slalom, it is therefore very important that you make the change for the next swing early, otherwise you will miss the next gate. With flexible poles continue

BIG FOOT

trying to get as close as possible to the pole as you pass it. You will achieve this if you move your upper body inside and 'through' the pole while your legs go 'over' the pole and only your BIG FOOT go 'round' the pole base. So that the gate pole does not 'wipe' you out, strike it out of the way with the outside of the arm before you come into contact with it.

By using the 'clearing' technique with the outside of the arm you will be running down an ideal line. It becomes more critical when you 'clear' away the pole with the shins. In the ideal case your upper body will thus always remain bent downhill. Only the legs swing round the pole. Using this technique on the giant slalom will allow you to gain a few metres.

Well, that's enough of the theory. In order to be on the podium for the next World Cup races you will need a lot of practice. BIG FOOT will give you an early opportunity to get to know the slalom in the professional sense. You will be even more concentrated when doing your gate training. Twisting and weaving in and out of the gates will be devoid of any spectacular crashes, and you will not need to turn yourself into a mountain climber to chase after lost skis. With BIG FOOT it does not take much energy to reposition dislodged gate poles. So, go ahead and use the opportunity to have a day doing the slalom on BIG FOOT - it will remain an everlasting experience.

10 "UP IN THE CLOUDS" – FLYING SCHOOL FOR 'JUMPERS' WITH SHOE SIZE 24 AND LARGER

Jumping is 'really cool' – it looks good ... and shows the spectators that the 'actor' possesses courage and skill. However, not least of all, do prevent an accident happening. You should get yourself well-schooled for it – practising jumping is the best way to improve your safety. Safety, in this sense, when you have to avoid unexpectedly an object or a person. Quick reaction and absolute control of the equipment help to prevent accidents. Furthermore, your eye must be on the constant lookout for unevenness in the ground – an absolute essential for planning your skiing line.

Besides the safety aspects, jumping – above all the feeling of flying – is a great fun thing. So that jumping, however, does not turn into a nightmare here are a few ground rules that must be observed:

1. Never jump over an escarpment or a hillock without knowing what it looks like on the other side – So, no flying by instruments!
2. Have someone stand on the brow of the jump area who will give an all clear.
3. When jumping a hillock for the first time go as slowly as possible and do a test jump for safety. Reaching up into the clouds comes later enough!
4. So that you do not end up flying through the air and catapulting onto your back, do not choose a hillock which has a sharp steep take-off. Flatter hillocks and moguls, where the ground beyond falls away steeper, are best.

Before we get onto aerial jumps, a word or two regarding the landing techniques – for the novice pilots amongst you. So that your landing will not look like that of an albatross, get yourself into a middle position. Backward or forward leaning postures tend to lead to a crash landing. As

BIGFOOT

soon as your feet feel contact with the ground again, let your legs give as if they were shock absorbers. What follows is a question of personal courage. Learning by doing is the watchword here. As with all jumping movements note that, whilst in the air, you maintain your body tension! And now, jump!

The Upright Jump

This is a jump with the body stretched all the way up. Again – tense your muscles and maintain your body tension during the flight phase. Stretch your arms out horizontally so that you can compensate better and keep your balance.

Jumping with a Change of Direction

During the flight phase your original direction is slightly changed. This is made to happen by slightly twisting the body whilst in the air, or by pushing one leg forward as you take-off.

Open Leg Jump

Open leg jumping is the first and simplest of jumps employing an additional element whilst in the air. You need some time to be able to execute this movement. It follows that the jump must take a higher trajectory so that you gain the time. The legs are pushed apart at the same time as you stretch up. Again, you should stretch out your arms horizontally to maintain your balance.

The 'Duffy' or Airwalk

Now we get really professional! The 'Duffy', or Airwalk, is a large jump into the new dimension of flying. During the aerial phase you stretch one leg forwards and the other backwards, bending it at the knee joint.

The Knees-Bend Jump

The body turns into a compact package, and in ideal cases your arms grasp your shins as your legs are pulled up.

Remember the 'water bomb' at the pool-side? Now we are jumping like that on our BIG FOOT. The legs are, however, this time stretched back down before we land and absorb the shock.

BIG FOOT

Open leg jump

Airwalk

Knees-bend jump

Jumping into voids

Jumping into Voids

This jump demands a large helping of courage and is extremely spectacular. The long flight phase allows one to execute various different trick elements in the air, one after the other. The important point is that the landing area must be 'schuss' type of ground. In this way the landing will not be too hard and the risk of injuring oneself will be minimal.

Naturally there are a lot more types of jumps and trick elements which one can try out on BIG FOOT. Names such as 'back scratcher' to 'Helicopter 360' fall to mind. In order to keep the BIG FOOT accident statistics down we are going to dispense with any further detailed explanations. One thing we must add is that if you can jump safely on BIG FOOT, you will equally be able to jump well on normal skis. The long planks forgive many a mistake in your body positioning – clumsily executed jumps will often come off with a reasonable landing. Nevertheless if you do have a slam on the long planks, the danger of an accident is considerably larger than on BIG FOOT.

11 THE SWING A LA BIG FOOT – CARVING ON BIG FOOT

"It is like riding a motor bike. Just before your footrest scrapes along the ground ... you lay the bike over into the turn further and further! A thought shoots suddenly through your head – if the outside foot does not come back under the body then there will be a wipe out. Your outside leg is almost fully stretched out; your weight is totally on your thigh. Your hips are close to the mountain side and your bottom is almost grazing along the ground; your inside arm grasps at the snow which sprays up ... and then your foot comes back under the body and you regain your balance. That's the BIG FOOT swing."

(Reinhold M.* - Stubai Glacier 1995).
* Name changed by the editors.

Carving is **the** innovation in contemporary winter sport. BIG FOOT can be quite an aid in digging into this world of experiences. The BIG FOOT swing can be included in the category of carving movements. Its execution and style lies somewhere between normal skiing and snowboarding. We speak of it in this way because it has been used by lots of BIG FOOT-ers earlier on, before carving became the rage. The swing turn can help you learn to do cfarving. You will experience a whole new feeling doing it – all due to the splendid running characteristics of your BIG FOOT. Here too there are a number of different ways of copying it, and everyone does it slightly differently. Nevertheless we are going to try and describe how you can do it here.

The principle characteristics of the swing are running on the edge (carving) and changing from the one edge to the other edge. It is dynamic and quick. There is no drifting, slipping, flat-spots or unweighting – only top speed all the time; and no change of this in the turn. These are the basics of the BIG FOOT swing in this sense. In order to bring the movement about you will need, initially, to get up to a relatively high speed. In this way you will guarantee that you will be able to get into the swing turn

BIG FOOT

BIGFOOT

providing you get onto the edges – a lot of this is due to the centre slim lines of your BIG FOOT. This develops into a quick stylish movement which, in its extreme form, leads to a quite radical way of skiing. Your balance in the turn reaches critical proportions i.e., you lean so far into the turn, using centrifugal force, that if it was not for your forward speed you would lose your balance and fall onto your side. Your body can lean over so far that it will be horizontal with the piste; you are almost balancing on the snow with your inner arm – just like snowboarding – and the outside leg is almost completely stretched out.

How do I get to try out this spectacular and uncompromising style?

There are two decisive factors: leave fear and anxiety at home, and make sure you have a good solid feeling on BIG FOOT. Other important factors are that you use a broad flat red run with not much 'traffic' – ideal conditions to try out the BIG FOOT swing.

The first step is to recognise when you are on the edges. Ski downhill and try, merely by edging, to make a turn. Watch your BIG FOOT as you do this. Your edge must 'cut' into the slope e.g., when your BIG FOOT is edged over so far, your partner (if you are skiing in pairs) can see the white underside running surface. A further point to notice is the snow which should be spraying up. The edging movement can be made easier if you adopt a low posture at the same time and place the weight of your body, or your arms, over the inside thigh.

Since your whole weight is now transferred to the inside, you can edge the outside BIG FOOT on your stretched out leg. You will immediately start to go into a turn. To get the outside BIG FOOT to edge properly you must feel that the inside of your anklebone (or the inside of the ski boot) is touching the snow. Your bottom is almost scraping along the ground, and because of the low posture adopted, a crash will not be painful at this low speed. This means that you can really go all out and risk a thing or two. If you are being pulled into the swing then you have mastered the most important phase of the BIG FOOT swing.

In order to be able to get into a steeper lean, and thus be on the right way to be able to do carving all the time, the next step is to ski a single swing, scribing a large radius. Ski downhill again but this time with a bit more speed. Get into the swing by holding out your arms as if they were wings of a plane and dip into the turn. Push your outside leg well out and at the end of the swing hold yourself up on the inside arm.

All you have to do now is to try out a swing in both directions. In this way you avoid creating a favourite side. You will soon notice that, by increasing your speed, you will be able to hold a good steep leaning posture. Similarly, you will soon be able to edge both BIG FOOT automatically, that is the outside edge of the inside BIG FOOT and the inside edge of the outer BIG FOOT.

So that you are able to resist the pressure, and still be able to ski sharper swing turns, at the time when the pressure comes on, you must 'go for it again'. You can do this by not only consciously resisting the pressure, but also by trying to push off with the BIG FOOT on the outside leg so that your lightly bent outside leg is now completely straightened. This movement automatically digs the edge in deeper. Sometimes however a manoeuvre like this will create such a force that you will be catapulted out of the swing turn.

Now you must try to do the opposite edging movement by swinging your hips over to the other side after the first turn, and thus start to be able to do one swing after the other. For the onlooker it appears as if you have made a short upward lifting movement, coupled with a deliberate unweighting, so that you have room for the hips to swing over. The

BIG FOOT

movement is, however, only completed when the hips have been pushed under the upper body as you bring across your balance. This all gives you the ability to drop into the new swing.

This short description of the movement above should assist you in becoming a 'flat-out BIG FOOT-er'.

As before we say that we are only putting experiences we ourselves have gained into suggestions. Bring your own variations into play and by doing so, have even more fun.

12 'FEET GONE TO SLEEP?' – NO THANK YOU! GETTING USED TO SKIING WITH BIG FOOT

In general it should have been clear by now to our readers, that this book is not about how to do certain movements in exact detail. Indeed BIG FOOT skiers should not succumb to trying to learn complete or stereotyped ways of doing things. We prefer to lead you to assimilate things – to create a dimension of experience and self-perception. This makes learning to ski with BIG FOOT a particularly exciting experience, which also is valid for normal skiing. There can be no one single component which is applicable to BIG FOOT. BIG FOOT has, above all, the advantage, when you are trying to attain your wish of accomplishment, that they are relatively risk free and easy to handle, thus allowing you to concentrate with no diversions. It is the diversionary aspect which causes us no longer to worry about ourselves – we only need to think about the equipment. "It is a bad workman who blames his tools!" You are simply able to correlate the features of the equipment and its uses with your feelings and your own perceptions.

The almost consuming concentration on the equipment reduces as ability increases. This is one of the reasons why we have devoted this chapter, in the main, to the expert. He has a greater need to busy himself with this subject, because he has already automated himself into the elementary mechanics of gliding and maintaining his balance. Despite this, this subject is important for every level of ability. This was our intention in writing 'The Alternative Beginner's Course', where we have covered the introduction of the intuitive feeling. Just as we pointed out in the section entitled 'Body Posture and Using the Board Edges', one can also 'feel' the biomechanical principles of steering into the swing – an opening to winter sports which offers much to the beginner. Read again the lines about the correlation of the body posture and the pressure on the sole of the foot. Exercises were included, which contribute to heightening your sensitivity and feeling for how the sole of the foot should work and the feed-back signs given as a result for BIG FOOT skiers. Your understanding of this subject material will lead automatically to a more

BIGFOOT

complete perception and will dispense with the reliance on only being able to 'see' things. Up to now, generally only lip service has been afforded to the feed-back signs from the nerves in the muscles and from the inside of your body, and from training to do with your sense of balance, noticing noises, as well as your perception on the skin of pressure, warmth or coldness.

In the following part, there are some exercises which serve to heighten your perception and give you an introduction to this subject.

Perceptiveness

As mentioned above, most of the observations which one makes are to do with the sense of vision. The connection means that this sense unavoidably forms the main perception in one's mind. "Did you **see** how he skis?" or "The mogul **looks** rather difficult and well-worn" – "Did you **see** the sheets of ice?"

Here are some exercises which will give you some new experiences, because they are rooted in various different senses.

First of all you should take it on yourself to no longer look at the ground in the assumption that this is the only way you are going to be able to move over it. The ground itself is capable of giving signs as feed-back which allows you to know what to do. The chain reaction does not run from head to toe – rather the opposite way round.

The first exercise: your partner holds up two, three or four fingers. He is standing about 20 metres downhill from you. You ski down to him calling out the number of fingers he is holding up. He changes the number and you call out to him what they are ... etc.

A further exercise (harder): skiing blindfolded. This serves to train your sense of balance. You 'sense' varying types of snow and your ears 'perceive' which way to go from directions given as well as hearing the sound of your BIG FOOT and their edges.

Ski downhill alongside your partner. One of you is blindfolded. To guide the other a ski stick is held out horizontally in front of the body, which the 'blind man' holds onto.

You can heighten the experience by skiing down a simple slope, without ski sticks, after trying out the exercise above. The 'blind man' goes off in front and the partner calls out which way to go and any changes of speed from behind. You will find out that both exercises require considerable confidence, but at the same time make you receptive to the use of the senses of hearing and touch.

Body Tension

The term 'body tension' means tensing all the muscles which are often easily neglected by BIG FOOT skiers and which cause involuntary movements, or an instability in your posture. In the following exercises we show how you can improve your body tension and its uses.

You can easily improve your feeling for body tension by getting together with two other partners. One of you tenses his body like a board and leans to one side. So that he does not fall over he is supported, as he leans over in his slanting position, by a partner who then thrusts him away over to the other side. The partner on that side supports him as he continues to hold his 'board-like' tenseness. If this movement is done several times it resembles a pendulum. The BIG FOOT are constantly being edged each time.

A further way to achieve perception is to try out extreme positions with a maximum forwards or backwards lean. This exercise is also best done with three people so that no-one lands up in the snow. Make note of the various different pressure points on the balls of the feet, the outsides of the feet, the calves and the shins when doing this exercise. This will give you feed-back information about your body position for later, and this serves to allow you to correct it yourself.

Stand normally with your BIG FOOT spread out at a hip's breadth. Now consciously tense all the muscles in your body one after the other:

Adopting a slightly forward leaning posture, start with the shins and calves moving up to the muscles of your backside and followed by the stomach muscles which you press outwards. Do not forget to take a breath. Finally tense your arm muscles and imagine you are carrying a barrel in front of you. Screw your hands up into fists.

After these exercises it is time to do some skiing – first of all using a fully tensed body and then, as a contrast, try it holding your muscles as loosely as possible.

By the way, raise your antenna, at least once, when you ski down undulating ground.
Here you should be able to decipher the differences between the two states of tenseness quite clearly. They can be used deliberately for different purposes (gaining your balance or jumping).

These exercises will help you recognise your body tension as being a considerable component for BIG FOOT skiing.

Breathing and Rhythm

The perception of your breathing will help you in a variety of situations. In general, very often we do not notice that we are breathing – at best a snort or two when we have exerted ourselves a lot. We should tune up this also, so that we can use our breathing to good effect and be able to influence our skiing rhythm.

Practise breathing from the stomach (diaphragm) standing still. When you breathe through the nose your stomach is pressed outwards. Breathing out slowly through the mouth, carry on until it appears that the stomach has automatically pulled itself inwards. You can lay your hand on your stomach to check this out.

For a second exercise execute a long swing turn. As you start the swing take a deep breath in, and as you sweep into the turn breathe out slowly, at the same time continually increasing the pressure on the outside BIG FOOT.

When all the air has gone the stomach automatically stretches forward and you breathe in again. You can combine all of this with a vertical movement – breathe out slowly as you go down, and breathe in as you bring your body explosively back up again.

This type of 'power skiing' has shown you how you can combine breathing with the radius of the swing turn.

You can also vary the frequency of breathing – large swing turns – quiet breathing rate; short swing turns – high breathing rate.

This last exercise represents a precursor to matching the ground to your skiing style. Practise doing a series (... say 3) of rhythmic swing turns – first a long one then a short one – matching your breathing to these.

Application

Perception and intuitive skiing can have a number of uses. Even by trying out the different exercises from the collection of games is a help e.g., the inside ski swing turn. When skiing freely you will often find yourself compelled to alter the radius of your swing turns. The breathing exercises, described above, now offer you the capability to match your breathing to the situation.

This chapter can only give you a first glimpse of the subject of perception. As you are faced with differing situations e.g., jumping, skiing in mogul terrain or doing a slalom, try to think about your 'inner swing' and apply it. Also, at the beginning of each new season, when you stand there on your BIG FOOT again, think through this subject. You will notice that it does help. Body tension, balance and breathing are all closely related with one another. If you give your attention to these three subject areas, you will be able continually to perfect your skiing style.

13 'GET into THE RHYTHM' on 'Large Feet!'

Rhythm is an expansive phenomenon of movement which opens up the way for us to express ourselves in a special sort of way. Just as in other types of active sport forms, BIG FOOT also possesses a specific rhythm and movement. That is to say it is characterised by a series of changes between phases of tension and relaxation. Within limitations these can vary individually or be changed according to your temperament. A prerequisite for this is that the rhythm for the specific sport in question can be perceived by the person trying to do it i.e., it can be felt. The necessary feeling for rhythm to do this is by no means only for people born with such a special talent for it. On the contrary it is an ability which every person has. The only thing is, they do not often realise that they can do it. This means:

The natural ability to be able to move rhythmically, thus achieving a really fun feeling, is in general achievable and can be learned, of course, particularly using BIG FOOT.

The following tips and exercises should give you an appropriate introduction for this. They have been developed and successfully put into practice during winter sports events comprising holiday groups and school classes.

The concept touches on two basic principles:
- Rhythmical execution of a movement is not only a topic for so-called 'experts'. BIG FOOT-ers are able to collect experience and get this feeling while already carrying out their first attempts at a change of direction.
- The feeling for rhythm and rhythmical movements themselves come from different directions or are learned and built on in a variety of ways. The movements come either from inside you intuitively, dependent on your own imagination, and take on a dynamic aspect,

or they stem from or get matched to influences from outside your body – from the environment around you. In the first instance the BIG FOOT skier creates his own rhythm by singing, talking out loud, by counting, or simply from his inner being i.e., not from audible sounds. In the second case the impulses come from music being played, or by members of the group calling out or clapping.

That's enough of the theory – more or less. Now, however, let's 'Move your body'!

'Move Your Body !' - Rhythmic Tuning and Warming-up

Start by marching on the spot with your BIG FOOT strapped on. Lift your legs well up off the snow and at the same time swing your arms up across the chest ('I am walking on the snow (with BIG FOOT)') You can now intensify the movement by placing your feet out wider – shoulder width – and keep marching on. Gradually your pulse rate will increase.

At the next marching step bend your right leg and at the same time push your left leg outwards. Your upper body moves over slightly to the right and you set your left leg softly down on the snow again.

Now for the other side. Move your upper body to the left; bend your left leg sharply upwards and stretch out your right leg. The movement resembles a swinging pendulum. As you change over from right to left bend your whole body down deeply. Since your arms are free and are only idly hanging about as you oscillate from one BIG FOOT to the other, in the next phase you can bring them into play as well. Move your upper body over to the right and at the same time stretch your left arm up over your head as an extension of your left leg and vice versa. Now the movement is complete and you oscillate both your arms and legs from right to left and from left to right ...

As a large group you can do these 'aerobic exercises' on your BIG FOOT, varying them as you wish, and get even more fun out of it by singing or counting, or by doing it to music coming from the loudspeakers in the lift station.

You can see from the picture on page 134, that one can do aerobics on BIG FOOT on sand as well as on snow.

Down the Mountain with a Rhythm

Once you have got yourself tuned in rhythmically for the day's fun we can go ahead. In pairs you ski off with the leading partner doing large swing turns (constant rhythm) while the second skier tries to imitate the leader (shadowing). As an aid, to accompany the rhythm, you can use words like 'in - out', 'up - down' or 'boom - boom' (use your imagination for others). You yourself can give these beat messages out or have some other member of the group do it. You could also count or sing a song together.

When skiing, if you have been able to achieve a stable rhythm beat, e.g., only long or short swing turns, now try to vary it by changing the type and sequence of turns. For example: three long, then three short. Call out the beat as you do them e.g., 'long, long, long' or 'short, short, short' and so on.

The rhythmical construction of swings can be varied using the time factor. You can vary between acceleration and deceleration – slowly executed swings, or rapidly executed swings. In this exercise you are working with a contrast (fast – slow), and this is a precursor to cross – country skiing and makes BIG FOOT skiing fun.

A further way, which is also suitable for beginners, is rhythmical synchronised skiing. On BIG FOOT this type of movement takes on the appearance of moving together, either in pairs or in larger groups, following one another or spread out in a line and all swinging in synchronisation. Try this out by following the movements of your partner.

It also makes a lot of fun to try to make up certain synchronised rhythms to follow. This form is a little more difficult than the first, but can be fascinating. As a pair, or in a group, you try to keep together as you ski along in synchronisation e.g., two short swings and then one long slow swing. During this you can either keep eye contact with your partner or count and call out to each other – 'short - short - long - short - short - long'; or '1, 2 whoops a daisy; 3-4 – whoops a daisy!' and so on. When doing this exercise it is all about the emphasis on tension and relaxing as well as the relative timing and change between 'putting on pressure' and 'relaxing pressure', and at the same time keeping in step with your partner or group.

Wherever you hear music being played (ski huts, ski-lifts etc.,) try to pick up the musical rhythm and translate this into your movements (gliding, swing turns, steps, jumps ...). You could take along a walkman with ear plugs and match your movements to the music of your choice. For safety reasons, however, you should leave one ear free while skiing like this so that you are to able perceive other sounds going on around you.

Training to do rhythmical movements is not intended to turn the BIG FOOT skier into 'a classy star'. It is more about increasing your fun, and to be successful in linking several swing turns together in rhythm. Other factors are the ability to work as a team with your partner or group; be able to change your rhythm at will but in control, and at the same time to be able to get your rhythm to match the ground over which you are skiing. In short – it is all about having fun playing with the variations of movements, with your partner and with the terrain.

BIG FOOT

At the end of a rhythmical day on the 'large feet' you can then go off further on your 'little feet' to take part in a 'little après BIG FOOT'.
Why not?

BIGFOOT

14 'FOOTSTEPS IN THE SAND?' – A PREVIEW

The world is becoming crazier and crazier – sport as well. Whoever said that BIG FOOT was only a winter sport will have to revise his thinking. We learned this when we took part for the first time in a BIG FOOT slalom on sand. Meanwhile it has become an everyday thing that one can snowboard on sand and ski on artificial slopes or in a hall. Well, why shouldn't you give yourself a fun break and be able to devote time to your new hobby at any time in the year? BIG FOOTing in the sand has made this possible.

In principle it is no different than doing it in the element you have already got used to – snow. So strap them on, and ... 1, 2, 3 off we go ...!

However your 'feet' should not necessarily be new ones. Because of the higher resistance caused by the sand, the skiing surface suffers considerably after one or two runs. You can get round this by screwing an artificial plastic plate to the surfaces of your BIG FOOT. This measure of course means that this set is then written off for your winter sport events, but it does mean that their life-span on sand will be considerably increased.

A word about the terrain. Most of the sand hills, whether they be artificially created or natural ones, have roughly the same gradient which makes your choice a little restricted. Another factor is the steep appearance of the slope you meet – but, because of the high resistance between the skiing surface and the sand that we mentioned earlier, the speed will not be that high – even when schussing.

You will feel a little shaky when you try it out on sand for the first time. Everything is somehow a little strange. Dressed in shorts and a T-Shirt you do not exactly get that winter feeling – however once you pick up speed ...! Because the sand 'drags' more than snow, to start with you should adopt a slightly backwards leaning posture. But not too far – you know why, do not you!? Pick up speed and try out a few things. You will be left with perhaps somewhat mixed feelings after your first run, but as you start your second one you will not be able to imagine ever having only done this in winter.

Should you 'just happen' to find a few slalom poles standing around doing 'nothing', you will experience immeasurable fun. Slams in sand are almost always not dangerous. Most of the times we experienced this type of mishap, the only result was the grating sound of sand in the teeth.

For five years now there has been an annual international Sand BIG FOOT Championship in the town of Hirschau in the Oberpfalz (Germany). For this event, they spray the sand with water in order to reduce resistance. The result is very noticeable.

On the whole an informal and very congenial event which gave us a great deal of fun – perhaps we'll see you there one day!?

LITERATURE

Adden, W. / Leist, K.H. / Petersen, U.	„Problemlösendes Lernen im Sport". In: Sportpädagogik. 2. Jg. 1978, H1.
Bauer, D.	„Wie Wissenschaft Bewegungserfahrung herstellen kann." In: Dietrich, K.; Landau, G. (Hg.) Annäherungen, Versuche, Betrachtungen. Bewegung zwischen Erfahrung und Erkenntnis. Sonderheft der Zeitschrift Sportpädagogik. Velbert o.J.
Brodtmann, D. / Landau. G.	„An Problemen lernen." In: Sportpädagogik 6/1982/3, 16-22.
Bucher, W.	1017 Spiel- und Übungsformen im Skifahren und Skilanglauf. Schorndorf 1992.
Deutscher Verband für das Skilehrwesen (Hg.)	Skilehrplan 1. Elementarschule- Grundschule. München BLV 1981. Skilehrplan 3. Skifahren in jedem Gelände, Skifahren in jedem Schnee. 5. Aufl. München BLV 1982. Skilehrplan 5. Theorie. 6. Aufl. München BLV 1979. Skilehrplan 8. Skiunterricht. München BLV 1987. Skilehrplan Band 1. 7. Aufl. München BLV 1994. Skilehrplan Band 3. 1. Aufl. München BLV 1995.
Dietrich, K. / Landau, G.	Sportpädagogik. Reinbek 1990.
Epple, M. / Weiß, E.	„Der Big Foot im Skikurs". In: Skilehrer 1/96, 23-27.
Gereke, A. / Spengemann- Bach, I.	„Skifahren mit Big Foot, Langlauf und Alpinski." In: Sportpädagogik 6/1993, 48-51.
Groddeck, N.	„Aspekte zu einer Theorie erfahrungsoffenen Lernens." In: Garlichs, A. /Groddeck, N. (Hg.). Erfahrungsoffener Unterricht. Freiburg 1978.
Kuchler, W.	„Skilauf alpin: Vom Gängelband zur Selbsterfahrung." In: Brettschneider, W.D. (Hg.). Sportunterricht 5-10, 159-181. München, Wien, Baltimore 1981 Skizirkus. Böblingen 1985. Die neue Skitechnik. Reinbek 1989, Ausgabe 1993.
Leist, K.-H. / Loibl, J.	Vom gefühlvollen Sich-Bewegen und seiner Vermittlung. In: Sportpädagogik 14 (1990) 4 , 19-25. „Zur bewegungspädagogischen Bedeutung von Körpererfahrung". In: Bielefeld, J. (Hg.) Körpererfahrung, Grundlagen menschlichen Bewegungsverhaltens. Göttingen 1986, 36-58.

LITERATURE

Maraun, H.-K.	„Erfahrung als didaktische Kategorie." In: Dietrich, K. /Landau, G. (Hg.). Annäherungen, Versuche, Betrachtungen. Bewegung zwischen Erfahrung und Erkenntnis. Sonderheft der Zeitschrift Sportpädagogik. Velbert o.J.
Müller, H.	Eltern Skibuch. Reinbek 1988.
Petanjek, H.	„Big Foot in der Wintersportwoche – mehr als nur ein lustiges Sportgerät." In: Leibesübung – Leibeserziehung. Heft 6 1994, 18f.
Rabenstein, R.	Lernen kann auch Spaß machen! 4. Auflage Münster 1992.
Rieder, H., / Balschbach, R./Payer, B.	Lernen durch Rhythmus, Aspekte eines musikalisch orientierten bewegungsrhythmischen Lehrkonzepts. Heidelberg 1991.
Ritter, M. / Pramann, U.	Faszination Snowboarding. München 1979.
Scherler, K.H.	Sensomotorische Entwicklung und materiale Erfahrung. Schorndorf 1975. „Bewegung und Spiel in der Eingangsstufe." In: Die Grundschule 1976, 8. Jahrgang.
Schock, K.K.	Ski Direct. Big Foot – Ergo – Alpinski. Köln 1995.